P9-CMW-693

Better Homes and Gardens®

celebrate the
SEASON®
2007

Meredith® Books
Des Moines, Iowa

Test Kitchen

Our seal assures you that every recipe in *Celebrate the Season* has been tested in the Better Homes and Gardens Test Kitchen. This means that each recipe is practical and reliable, and meets our high standards of taste appeal. We guarantee your satisfaction with this book for as long as you own it.

All of us at Meredith Books are dedicated to providing you with information and ideas to enhance your home. We welcome your comments and suggestions. Write to us at: Meredith Books Editorial Department, 1716 Locust St., Des Moines, IA 50309–3023. *Celebrate the Season* is available by mail. To order editions from past years, call 800/439-7159.

Cover Photographs:
Jay Wilde

Front Cover Project: Minty Fresh Centerpiece, page 111

Back Cover Projects:
Thanksgiving Tabletop, page 14
Lid It Up, Up, Up, page 49
Easygoing Appetizer Party, page 104
Miniskirt Purse, page 142

Better Homes and Gardens

Celebrate the Season 2007

Editor: Kristin Bienert
Food Editor: Jessica Saari
Contributing Editor: Susan Banker
Contributing Food Editor: Winifred Moranville
Contributing Recipe Editor: Joyce Trollope
Contributing Recipe Developers: Carrie E. Holcomb, Joyce Lock
Contributing Art Director/Graphic Designer: Catherine Brett
Copy Chief: Terri Fredrickson
Copy Editor: Kevin Cox
Publishing Operations Manager: Karen Schirm
Senior Editor, Asset and Information Manager: Phillip Morgan
Edit and Design Production Coordinator: Mary Lee Gavin
Editorial Assistant: Cheryl Eckert
Book Production Managers: Pam Kvitne, Marjorie J. Schenkelberg, Rick von Holdt, Mark Weaver
IC Operators: Tony Goforth, Don Atkinson
Contributing Copy Editor: Judy Friedman
Contributing Proofreaders: Karen Grossman, Gretchen Kauffman, Jeanée Ledoux
Test Kitchen Director: Lynn Blanchard
Test Kitchen Product Supervisor: Jill Moberly

Meredith Books
Editor in Chief: Gregory H. Kayko
Executive Director, Design: Matt Strelecki
Managing Editor: Amy Tincher-Durik
Executive Editor: Jennifer Darling
Senior Editor/Group Manager: Jan Miller
Senior Associate Design Director: Ken Carlson

Editorial Director: Linda Raglan Cunningham
Executive Director, Marketing: Kevin Kacere
Executive Director, New Business Development: Todd M. Davis
Executive Director, Sales: Ken Zagor
Director, Operations: George A. Susral
Director, Production: Douglas M. Johnston
Director, Marketing & Publicity: Amy Nichols
Business Director: Jim Leonard

Vice President and General Manager: Douglas J. Guendel

Better Homes and Gardens Magazine
Editor in Chief: Gayle Goodson Butler
Deputy Editor, Home Design: Oma Blaise Ford
Deputy Editor, Food and Entertaining: Nancy Wall Hopkins

Meredith Publishing Group
President: Jack Griffin
Senior Vice President: Karla Jeffries
Vice President, Corporate Solutions: Michael Brownstein
Vice President, Creative Services: Ellen de Lathouder
Vice President, Manufacturing: Bruce Heston
Vice President, Consumer Marketing: David Ball
Consumer Product Associate Marketing Director: Steve Swanson
Consumer Product Marketing Manager: Wendy Merical
Business Manager: Darren Tollefson

Meredith Corporation
Chairman of the Board: William T. Kerr
President and Chief Executive Officer: Steve Lacy

In Memoriam: E. T. Meredith III (1933–2003)

Copyright © 2007 by Meredith Corporation. Des Moines, Iowa.
First Edition.
All rights reserved.
Printed in the United States of America.
ISSN: 1098-0733
ISBN: 978-0-696-23496-5

Anticipation

Anticipation for the holiday season began when I was just 4 years old at my brother's school Christmas concert. Propped on Dad's knee, I had the best seat in the house.

Afterward I stood in a long line of kids as Mom fussed with my hair bow. Then I saw him: a kind-looking man dressed in red. He had a beard bigger than I had ever seen and boots shinier than Dad's best work shoes.

Santa talked softly to me as if he really DID know me. He was purely magical. I hugged him before I climbed down and couldn't wait to get home to help Mom bake cookies for Santa's visit that weekend.

Ever since that special moment, I have entered the holiday season with great anticipation. From Thanksgiving to New Year's Day, I do everything I can to make similar feel-special memories for my family and friends. That's

the purpose of this book: to give you festive decorating projects, delicious can-do recipes, and wondrous gift ideas that make the season incredibly bright. So here's to you and all the eagerly awaited magic you'll provide this holiday season. Let the merriment begin!

Sue Banker

Sue Banker

3

■ Create a showy, snowy centerpiece or end table decoration by arranging a mix of snowflake and ball ornaments, white candles, and beaded snowballs in a clear pedestal dish filled with white aquarium pellets. Place the bowl on silver fabric covered with iridescent white mesh. A trio of snowflake ornaments at the pedestal base finishes the look for a glistening wintry presentation.

table *of* contents

setting the stage

Transform your home into a holiday haven with easy decorating projects that sing with warmth and joy. Try these ideas for indoors and out and discover fun, new ways to celebrate in style.

gathering together

It's one of the most wonderful benefits of the season—spending time with people that mean the most to you. Treat your guests to unforgettable parties, fantastic foods, fun decorating themes, and little forget-me-nots that will make them feel as special as they are.

giving from the heart

Tailor gifts to suit your family and friends this year. Handmade surprises range from handsome desk accessories to playful kitchen hot pads, towels, and a recipe box that is too cute to ever put away in the cupboard. And what to give to someone who has everything? Food gifts that taste too good for words!

just for kids

Inspire the little ones to get creative by making candy houses, easy-paint mugs, supercool ornaments, and snowman cards that use suckers and potato-print backgrounds.

In a Twinkling
Easy projects you can make in an evening's time.

5

SETTING the STAGE

Let the spirit of the holiday season fill your heart and home. Feel-good, easy-does-it decorations lead the way from glorious autumn through tree-trimming time.

7

meaningful messages

Greet family and friends with heartfelt words and pretty autumn accents. Indoors and out these colorful decorations make lasting impressions.

tree of thanks

What You'll Need...

- tree branch
- handheld hedge clippers
- butter tub
- cement
- water
- disposable container
- stirring utensil
- hot-glue gun and glue sticks
- chickpeas or dried beans
- spray primer
- orange spray paint
- clear spray sealer
- orange glitter
- scissors
- decorative container, silk leaves, and rocks
- papers in green and gold
- paper trimmer
- glue
- marking pen
- shower curtain clips

Invite family and friends to write messages of thanks for all to see. This sharing tree shimmers with personal feelings as well as autumn colors. Chickpeas coat the branches with the look of berries, while paint and glitter add a festive finish.

1. Trim a dry dead branch to the desired size and shape using hedge clippers. If needed, combine several small branches.

2. Choose a container, such as a butter tub, that can be hidden in a decorative container and filled with cement.

3. Following the instructions on cement package, mix cement in a separate disposable container. Pour the cement into the butter tub.

4. Insert the branch base into the center of the cement-filled tub. Tap the sides of the tub until the branch sits firmly in cement. Allow cement to dry.

5. Use a hot-glue gun to adhere chickpeas or dried beans randomly to the branch, using as many as desired.

6. In an outdoor area spray the branch with primer. Spread extra chickpeas on newspaper and spray them with primer. Let the paint dry.

7. Spray the branch and chickpeas with orange paint. Let dry.

8. Spray one section at a time with clear sealer. Quickly sprinkle orange glitter into wet sealer. Let dry. Repeat this process until entire branch and chickpeas are glittered. Place the weighted tree into decorative container.

9. Place decorative rocks around the branch base until the cement is covered. Sprinkle extra chickpeas onto the rocks.

10. Trim silk leaves from stems. Coil the wired ends and hang on tree.

11. Trim 2-inch squares of green paper and 1¾-inch squares of gold paper. Center and glue the gold paper onto the green paper. Ask family members to use a marking pen to write thanks-filled messages on the squares. Use shower curtain clips to hang the messages from the branches.

12. Leave extra colored squares around the tree base for guests to add more messages to the tree.

What You'll Need...

- [ ] photograph
- [ ] glass hurricane
- [ ] 8½×11-inch sheet of white vellum
- [ ] wavy rotary cutter or decorative-edge scissors
- [ ] crafts knife
- [ ] 2 sheets of 8½×11-inch peach striped vellum
- [ ] spray adhesive, such as Craft Bond
- [ ] brown eyelets
- [ ] eyelet tool
- [ ] 3 brass maple leaf charms
- [ ] glue dots
- [ ] ribbons in peach, brown, and ivory
- [ ] ivory candle

smiles all aglow

Copy a family photo onto vellum and watch the light illuminate the special people in your life.

1 Determine the photograph size to fit the hurricane. Color-copy the photograph onto a sheet of white vellum.

2 Use a wavy rotary cutter or decorative-edge scissors to cut out the photograph, leaving a ½-inch border of white vellum around all sides.

3 Use a crafts knife to cut an opening the exact size of the photograph into one sheet of peach striped vellum, centering the opening on the sheet.

4 Secure the photograph onto the back side of the peach vellum by centering it in the opening. Place spray adhesive on the front side of the white border of the photograph and press it onto the back of the peach vellum. The picture will show through the opening. The wavy border will show up once the candle is lit.

5 Wrap the two sheets of peach vellum around the glass hurricane, overlapping evenly on each side.

6 Secure the two sheets of peach vellum to each other by placing eyelets evenly where the two sheets will overlap when placed on the hurricane. Once secure, the round sleeve of vellum should be the exact size of the hurricane. Slide the paper onto the hurricane.

7 Embellish the hurricane by attaching the three leaf charms centered below the photograph using glue dots. Using the three colors of ribbon, tie a bow around the base of the hurricane.

8 Place an ivory candle in the hurricane and light.

Note: For safety reasons, never leave burning candles unattended.

welcoming trio

Turquoise beads and ribbon lend Southwestern flair to Indian corn. Hung from a stick, this fall decoration can be crafted in just minutes.

1 If cornhusks are discolored and wrinkled, place in solution of 1 cup each of bleach and hot water. Let the husks soak approximately one hour until they lighten and look clean. Rinse and shape the husks. Let drip-dry.

2 Cut a ribbon length to wrap around each ear of corn. Apply small amounts of hot glue and wrap ribbon around corn. Secure the ends with dots of hot glue.

3 Cut a piece of wire 24 inches long. Leaving a 2-inch tail, wrap one end of the wire tightly around the stem of one husk several times until secure. Repeat until all of the ears are connected.

4 String beads onto the remaining wire, leaving 2 inches at the end free of beads. Twist the wire ends together securely and fold them into the husks. Cut an additional 12-inch piece of wire. Use pliers to fold over one end slightly so beads cannot fall off. Bead the wire and secure the end in the same fashion.

5 Use wire cutters to remove pins or earring backs from jewelry. Hot-glue jewelry pieces to centers of ribbon.

6 Wrap the hanging wire around a stick. Shape the 12-inch beaded wire into a loose spiral. Fold it in half and hang it from one end of the stick.

What You'll Need...

- Indian corn
- bleach
- hot water
- scissors
- turquoise ribbon
- hot-glue gun and glue sticks
- 22-gauge wire
- wire cutters
- assorted beads in turquoise and other colors that will fit onto wire
- pliers
- 3 pieces of old jewelry, such as earrings and pins
- stick

11

bittersweet basket

↶ Sheer wire screen forms easily into a basket shape ready to hold autumn's bounty. A ring of bittersweet adds glorious color to the arrangement.

What You'll Need...

- [ ] leather gloves
- [ ] 4 feet of 24-inch-wide wire screen
- [ ] beading wire
- [ ] wire cutters
- [ ] spray primer, such as Kilz
- [ ] spray paints in orange and lime green
- [ ] hedge balls, gourds, or small pumpkins
- [ ] bittersweet

1 Wear leather gloves to prevent scratches while handling the screen. Fold in one end of the screen approximately 1 inch to hide the sharp edge.

2 Shape the screen into a circle with the folded edge on the outside. Overlap it approximately 2 inches.

3 Weave beading wire in and out of the screen, sewing a seam to connect the two ends and making a secure loop of screen. Tie the ends securely.

4 Tuck and fold the bottom of the screen together to form it into a basket shape. Secure it together firmly, weaving beading wire in and out of the screen.

5 In a well-ventilated work area, spray the entire screen shape with a light coat of primer. Let dry.

6 Spray spots of orange paint onto the inside and outside of the screen shape. Spray the remainder of the screen with lime green paint. Let dry.

7 Roll the screen from the top down several times to create a cuff. Touch up with more paint if needed. Let dry.

8 Fill the wire basket with hedge balls, gourds, or small pumpkins. Wrap a vine of bittersweet around the cuff and tuck sprigs inside the basket. Secure the vine using small pieces of wire if needed.

13

please join us

Thanksgiving is a time to gather together to be ever grateful for the gift of family. As guests draw to the table, delight them with breathtaking place settings and a centerpiece fitting for the long-awaited dinner of the year.

pomegranate candlescape

〰 With a straw wreath for a base, this pomegranate and prairie grass ring makes a pretty frame for a field of candlesticks dancing center stage.

What You'll Need...

- [ ] 12-inch round straw wreath form
- [ ] brown raffia
- [ ] scissors
- [ ] 9 glittered artificial pomegranates
- [ ] 2-inch-wide plaid ribbon
- [ ] yellow-dyed prairie grass
- [ ] sheer ⅝-inch-wide gold ribbon
- [ ] 4-inch wood floral picks
- [ ] glass cake stand
- [ ] 7 brass candleholders in a variety of heights
- [ ] 8-inch tapered candles in burnt orange color
- [ ] candle putty (optional)

1 Wrap the straw wreath with several strands of brown raffia, knotting on the inside or bottom of the wreath.

2 Press the pomegranate stems evenly spaced into the wreath top.

3 Wrap lengths of plaid ribbon around the wreath, covering the areas between the pomegranates.

4 Break off a variety of lengths of prairie grass and press them into the wreath around the pomegranates. The prairie grass should overlap to create texture and add volume.

5 Tie a variety of lengths of gold craft ribbon bows and affix them to the 4-inch wooden floral picks.

6 Press the floral picks into the wreath form, filling in around the pomegranates and prairie grass.

7 Place the decorated wreath onto the glass cake stand. Arrange the brass candleholders in the center of the wreath on the cake stand.

8 Place the tapered candles into the candleholders. Use candle putty to hold them in place if necessary.

9 Tie a plaid ribbon bow around the base of the cake stand. For safety reasons, never leave burning candles unattended.

Note: For safety reasons, never leave burning candles unattended.

15

beribboned napkin rings

◠ Dress up a woven napkin ring with ribbon tails peeking from the center of a green glass disk.

What You'll Need...

- ☐ ¾-inch-wide plaid ribbon
- ☐ scissors
- ☐ round natural wicker napkin rings
- ☐ green glass bead disks
- ☐ sheer ⅝-inch gold craft ribbon cut into 12-inch lengths

1 Cut a plaid ribbon for each napkin ring 7 inches longer than the circumference of the ring. Wrap each ring with a measured length of ribbon. Thread the ends through the center of a green disk.

2 Wrap each end of ribbon around opposite sides of the green disk and bring them back through the center of the disk.

3 Tie a small bow with a 12-inch length of sheer gold ribbon. Attach the bow to the napkin ring by tying the ends of the plaid ribbon in a knot in the center of the bow.

harvest table runner

◠ Bring glorious autumn color to the table center with pieced squares of silk and coordinating plaid ribbons.

What You'll Need...

- ☐ scissors; tape measure
- ☐ sewing machine
- ☐ needle and thread
- ☐ ¼ yard each of 7 different silk fabrics in shades of gold, tan, green, copper, and brown
- ☐ 21×36-inch piece of backing fabric
- ☐ 3¼ yards of ¾-inch-wide plaid satin ribbon
- ☐ two 1¾-yard lengths of double-faced ⅝-inch-wide satin ribbon
- ☐ ¾ yard of ⅜-inch-wide plaid satin ribbon

1 Cut twenty-eight 6-inch squares from the different shades of silk fabric.

2 Piece together four blocks across and seven blocks down using a ½-inch seam.

3 With right sides facing, center pieced top over backing fabric and stitch around outside edge with ½-inch seam, leaving an opening for turning.

4 Trim seam allowance to ¼ inch and trim corners. Turn to right side and stitch opening closed.

5 Cut three lengths of ribbon the length of the runner plus the seam allowance. Cut six lengths of ribbon the width of the runner plus seam allowance.

6 Weave the ribbons on top of runner seams, turning under at the ends. Stitch to secure. Machine- or hand-stitch a few stitches at woven intersections to secure.

What You'll Need...

- table knife
- 2-inch plastic foam balls
- marbles or washers to weigh down the balls
- 2-inch-wide plaid ribbon cut in 14-inch strips (2 strips per place card holder)
- scissors
- wheat
- floral wire
- wire cutters
- brown raffia
- cream-color cardstock
- small paper punch
- paper leaf embellishments
- glue dots

let's wheat

🍂 Make each person at your Thanksgiving table feel special with a place card hanging gracefully from a single stalk of wheat nestled in a pretty satin-covered ball.

1 Use a table knife to shave off a small slice from each foam ball so it sits flat and does not roll.

2 Press a marble or washer into the flat side of each foam ball to provide extra stability for the place card holders to sit on the table.

3 Place two lengths of plaid ribbon overlapping in an X on a flat surface. Place the foam ball, flat side down, onto the center of the ribbon X.

4 Cut a stalk of natural wheat about 2 inches below the bud. Press the wheat stem into the top center of the foam ball so just the wheat is poking out.

5 Bring the edges of the plaid ribbon up around the wheat stem, wrapping the entire foam ball in ribbon. Tie the ends together with a short length of floral wire.

6 Tie three or four stands of brown raffia around the floral wire. Trim the tails of the raffia if desired.

7 Cut the cardstock into small rectangles. Punch a hole in the corner of each cardstock rectangle. Write a guest's name on each card.

8 Embellish the cards with a paper leaf by securing to the cards with glue dots.

9 Hang each name card by slipping it onto a single stalk of wheat.

cattail crazy

Beaded, painted, or glittered, dried cattails go from ditch to decoration in just a few easy steps.

beaded beauties

✍ Here's an idea that couldn't be simpler. Slip glass beads onto skinny cattail points to add dots of color to a natural bouquet.

What You'll Need...
- vase
- unpopped corn
- cattails
- colorful glass beads with holes large enough to fit cattail stems

1 Fill the vase half full with unpopped corn. Arrange several cattails in the vase, fanning out to give space between them.

2 Gently slip one or more glass beads onto the top points of the cattail stems until the beads cannot be pushed further.

20

color burst

〜 Seasonally painted cattail leaves and heads combine artistically into a wreath that will last the entire fall season.

What You'll Need...

- wire wreath form
- large piece of cardboard
- pencil
- crafts knife
- cutting surface
- hot-glue gun and glue sticks
- small cattails, at least 24
- small acorn cap
- white acrylic or inexpensive latex paint
- paintbrush
- kraft paper
- scissors
- acrylic paints in red, orange, yellow, and purple
- 250 cattail leaves

1 Place the wire form on the cardboard and trace just inside the edge of the inner opening.

2 Trim cardboard slightly larger than drawn circle. Use a knife to cut out the shape.

3 Glue the cardboard to the back side of wreath form with hot-glue gun.

4 Choose approximately 24 cattails about same size. Dip acorn cap and each cattail in white latex paint as shown in Photo A, *right*. Brush off excess paint and let dry, standing cattail tips on kraft paper as shown in Photo B. Trim off little beads of paint on the tips.

5 Paint 16 cattails and one acorn cap red. Paint eight cattails yellow. Using a wall to brace cattails, let dry standing on tips. Paint a second coat if needed.

6 Gather a bundle of approximately 250 cattail leaves. They should be starting to dry out, not too green, yet not too dry and brittle.

7 Paint approximately 200 leaves orange and let dry. Paint a second coat if needed. Let dry.

8 Paint approximately 50 leaves purple. Let dry.

9 Arrange red cattails onto wreath form first. Glue onto the cardboard with hot glue. Let cool.

10 Arrange orange leaves. Trim each to approximately the same length to fit from the center to outer edge of wreath. Continue to add leaves, gluing from the outer edge to the center until wreath is covered.

11 Add purple leaves. Glue some from the center outward on top of the orange. These should be trimmed shorter than the orange leaves. Glue a few evenly spaced on the back, keeping approximately the same length as shown in Photo C.

12 Trim the yellow cattails to the same length and glue eight on top of purple leaves from center outward. Glue the red acorn cap in the center of the wreath.

A

B

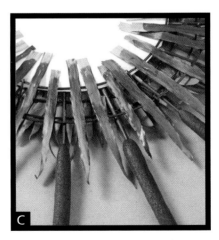

C

glitter and a gourd

 Tuck glittered cattails and autumn flowers in a natural dried gourd vase adorned with gilded leaves.

1. For vase place two dry or semidry leaves between the pages of a heavy book until they are very flat.

2. Choose a gourd with solid uniform base. Use a nonpermanent marker to draw a cut line onto gourd. Saw off the top portion of gourd along the marked line. Sand the cut edge smooth.

3. Remove the insides from the gourd. Soak and scrub the outside of gourd with hot soapy water, bleach, and a scouring pad. Use the blade of a nonserrated knife to remove mold and tough spots. Let dry.

4. Use a disposable paintbrush to apply wood stain to outside of gourd. Wipe with cloth rag and let dry.

5. Use a soft brush to apply foil adhesive to front side of leaves as shown in Photo A, *right*. Remove small hook from the wooden curtain rod ring. Apply adhesive to it. Paint the cut edge of gourd with adhesive also. Let dry just until tacky.

6. Gently lay sheets of leafing onto adhesive areas on leaves, gourd, and ring. Wipe away excess foil with a clean, dry paintbrush as shown in Photo B. Coat all foiled areas with clear sealer. Let dry.

7. Apply one coat of rubber cement to back of leaves and one coat onto the gourd where you want to position the leaves, covering more than enough area. Let dry until tacky but not wet.

8. Apply leaf to rubber cemented area. Note that this is not repositionable. Once put down it cannot be moved. Rub off all extra rubber cement that remains on the gourd.

9. Apply a small amount of wood glue to one side of the ring and attach to the bottom of the gourd so it sits securely as shown in Photo C. Let dry.

10. Turn gourd upside down and apply a generous amount of wood glue to the inside of the ring for extra stability. Let dry.

11. Paint cattails with a generous amount of matte decoupage medium. Sprinkle pink glitter into wet decoupage medium. Let dry standing upright in a vase.

12. Paint cattail stems with gold acrylic paint. Lay cattail leaves on newspaper and spray with gold spray paint. Let dry.

13. Arrange cattails and leaves in gourd vase. If the gourd needs some weight to support the cattails without tipping, place a few small rocks or unpopped corn in the bottom of the vase.

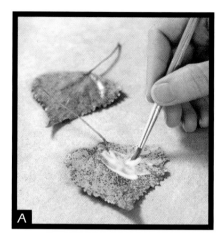

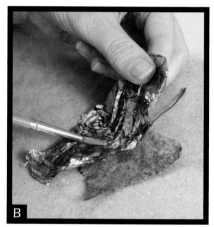

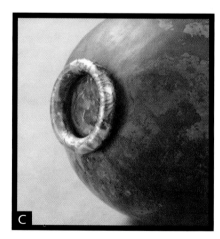

22

What You'll Need...

- [ ] dry or semidry leaves
- [ ] heavy book
- [ ] dried gourd
- [ ] nonpermanent marker
- [ ] saw
- [ ] sandpaper
- [ ] bleach and hot, soapy water
- [ ] scouring pad
- [ ] nonserrated knife
- [ ] disposable paintbrush
- [ ] wood stain
- [ ] soft cloth rag
- [ ] small soft paintbrushes
- [ ] foil adhesive
- [ ] wooden curtain rod ring
- [ ] red variegated gold leafing
- [ ] clear sealer
- [ ] rubber cement
- [ ] wood glue
- [ ] cattails
- [ ] matte decoupage medium
- [ ] pink glitter
- [ ] vase
- [ ] gold acrylic spray paint
- [ ] newspaper
- [ ] gold spray paint
- [ ] small rocks or unpopped corn (optional)

▶ **Sew a Crop** Simple wheat stitches transform a plain woven mat into one that brings autumn's bounty to the table. Add a border of running stitches and scrapbooking brads to complete the edge and then back with felt. For stitch diagrams, turn to page 157.

In a Twinkling

fall into it

◀ **Mosaic Master** Visit your crafts store to find a colored gourd and tiny pieces of glistening glass to embellish it. Plan out a simple pattern and hot-glue the mosaic squares in place. To keep horizontal patterns neat and aligned, place a large rubber band around the gourd to use as a guide.

Pinecone Tassel A simply made yarn tassel becomes an autumn ornament with the addition of tiny pinecones. Use brown suede lacing to tie the textural yarn. Wrap the tassel top with lacing as well, leaving long tails. Hot-glue pinecones as shown for a pretty finish.

Raffia Wraps Tie raffia around chunky candles to add interest and dimension. To really spruce things up, adhere a trio of pinecones to each candle using glue dots. Arrange the candles in an open wooden drawer or box and fill it in with more pinecones, bittersweet, nuts, or dried beans.

Go with the Grain A wood canister and cutting block are natural solutions to show off an autumn floral arrangement. If the canister doesn't have a watertight liner, simply slip a plastic cup or food storage container inside before adding blooms.

25

nature's gifts

Transform treasures found on a nature walk
into amazing curiosities for the holiday season.

all that glitters

Nestle tea lights in Epsom salts to multiply flickering candlelight. Flocked sticks stand at attention around the tiny campfire.

What You'll Need...

- [ ] large papier-mâché container in an interesting shape, such as holly
- [ ] white spray primer
- [ ] sticks
- [ ] saw
- [ ] hot-glue gun and glue sticks
- [ ] spray paint in light green
- [ ] clear matte sealer
- [ ] white fine glitter
- [ ] white puff paint for fabric
- [ ] paintbrush
- [ ] heat gun
- [ ] Epsom salts
- [ ] tea lights

1 Spray the outside and the inside of the papier-mâché container with white primier. Let dry.

2 Gather clean, dry sticks. They should be fairly straight to glue onto the container.

3 Saw off the sticks to roughly match or extend beyond the container height.

4 Hot-glue sticks around outside of container. Continue until the container is completely covered.

5 Lightly spray the sticks with light green. Let dry.

6 Spray clear matte sealer generously over sticks, one section at a time.

7 While the sealer is still wet, sprinkle with white glitter. Repeat to cover all sticks. Let dry.

8 Generously coat the stick tops with at least a ⅛-inch-thick layer of white puff paint. Use a brush to paint lightly down the sides of sticks and cover the inside of the box down at least 1 inch. Sprinkle with white fine glitter. Let dry 24 hours.

9 To puff the paint, apply heat with heat gun according to directions on paint. Repeat until all paint is puffed. If you desire more dimension, add more paint, repeating Steps 8 and 9.

10 Fill the container with Epsom salts. Fill up to 1 inch from the top.

11 Place metal-lined tea lights into salt gravel. For safety reasons, never leave burning candles unattended.

Note: For safety reasons, never leave burning candles unattended.

27

tree farm

Cone-shape shells mimic the shape of Christmas trees. Top the miniature trees with small starfish, glittered if desired, for the crowning glory.

What You'll Need...

- [ ] 1 large shell for dress
- [ ] 2 matching shells for wings
- [ ] 1 shell for face
- [ ] 1 shell for halo
- [ ] pencil
- [ ] drill and tiny bit
- [ ] acrylic iridescent paints
- [ ] waxed paper
- [ ] water and round paintbrush
- [ ] toothpick
- [ ] strong adhesive, such as E6000
- [ ] scissors
- [ ] cardboard
- [ ] white glue
- [ ] tiny starfish
- [ ] glitter
- [ ] tiny colored shells
- [ ] beads
- [ ] nylon string

heaven sent

Delicate shells in all shapes and sizes lend personality to a tiny angel ornament.

1 When choosing shells, make sure they fit together well, such as checking that the wings can be easily placed under the dress. Arrange shells together how you want them to be glued. Determine where to inset thread for hanging. Mark with a pencil.

2 Drill tiny holes where marked using a tiny drill bit.

3 If you want to enhance the color of the shells, apply a thin coat of acrylic paint. These shells are naturally pink and golden but also are painted. Lay waxed paper onto the work surface. Dilute the paint by mixing equal parts of water and paint. Brush on a thin coat and let dry. Iridescent, metallic yellow and pink were used on these shells.

4 Use a toothpick and adhesive to affix pieces together. Glue the wings onto the dress first, tucking the edges of the wing shells under the dress.

5 Glue the face to the halo. Then glue that piece onto the dress. Use a good amount of adhesive to get it to hold well; it will be covered up with tiny shells. Let set until firm.

6 Cut a small piece of cardboard to cover just a portion of the back side, especially where everything joins together. Apply a generous amount of adhesive to the cardboard and attach to the back to add stability to the piece. Let dry.

7 Use white glue to coat the starfish. While the glue is wet, sprinkle with glitter. Adhere tiny shells in a bouquet arrangement using white glue.

8 Trim the edges with white glue, add beads, and sprinkle with glitter. Let dry. Glue the starfish to the halo.

9 Tie the nylon string onto angel wings to hang.

a wreath with presence

Break out of the traditional holiday box and create a wreath that greets guests with presents. Embellish an evergreen ring with gift boxes dressed in holiday papers and add to the joy with shiny ornaments and bows.

deck the door

Sprinkle a little of Santa's magic on a plain purchased wreath. Flocked, fresh, dried, or medallion—choose the festive look you like.

felted holly

〰 Wool leaves and a trio of yarn-ball berries make a striking focal point for a fluffy flocked wreath.

To make the accent, enlarge and trace the holly pattern on *page 157* and cut out the shape. Trace around the holly pattern three times onto the paper side of fusible webbing. Cut out each leaf design, leaving a ¼-inch border of paper around the design. Following the instructions on the package, iron the fusible leaves onto green wool felt. Cut out the leaves and fuse onto three additional pieces of green wool felt. Cut out the holly leaf shapes. Zigzag-stitch a border on each leaf.

Twist pipe cleaners together to create a stem and veins for each leaf. Make each stem approximately 5 inches longer than the leaf to secure to the wreath. Zigzag-stitch the pipe cleaner stems and veins to each leaf.

Make the berries by securing one end of red wool yarn to a plastic foam ball and using a short length of red floral wire bent in the shape of a U. Wrap the ball with red yarn until covered. Secure the yarn end with another wire U. Make a "stem" for each berry by cutting a 10-inch length of red floral wire. Thread the wire through several strands of yarn covering each foam ball and twist to secure the wire.

Attach the berries and leaves to the wreath by twisting the wire stems around the wreath.

drum up attention

〰 A wooden nutcracker and pair of drumsticks are all you need to bring rum-pum-pum appeal to a dried wreath. Choose a fellow with a drum in hand to carry the theme. The trims mount easily to a twig wreath using crafts wire.

door decor

〜 A tall tin with a lid makes a great container for greens. Drill holes into each side of the tin and attach a decorative rope hanger. Fill the tin with greenery and berry picks, tucking the lid into the arrangement. Hold the lid in place with poster putty.

pinecone star

〜 Cut cardboard into a star shape and you have the base to make a stunning star wreath. Hot-glue pinecones to cover the edges, then fill in the center with more. Tie a trio of ribbons into a generous bow, leaving long tails. Accent the ribbon bow with a berry pick or two. Hot-glue the cluster to the star's center as a focal point, shaping the ribbon tails into spirals, if desired.

merry medallion

〜 A ceiling medallion is sure to be noticed when it's transformed into an ornate front door wreath. Spray paint the elaborate hardware-store find with a coat of black and let it dry. Use your favorite shade of green to spray paint the top coat, allowing the crevices to remain dark. When dry, hang the wreath from 3-inch-wide coordinating ribbon.

time to trim

From banisters to bookcases and Christmas tree branches, get ready to deck the halls with colorful symbols of the season.

tasseled trims

Scrapbook papers and recycled greeting card fronts are scaled for big impact on classic box ornaments.

What You'll Need...

- tracing paper
- pencil
- scissors
- 12-inch square of decorative scrapbooking cardstock to make 8x4¾-inch boxes
- assorted holiday cards to fit design
- assorted scrapbook paper
- glue stick
- awl
- narrow cord and tassel
- extra-long large-eye needle
- ribbons

1 Trace the pattern on *page 157* onto tracing paper. Cut out the pattern and use it to cut shape from cardstock. Score paper with scissors on indicated lines.

2 Cut out designs from holiday cards to fit front of box ornament. Add border of scrapbook paper under design for embellishment as desired.

3 Fold on score lines and glue into box shape. Fold down top and bottom curves. Mark center of top and bottom.

tag, you're it

4 Use an awl to pierce a small hole through centers of both layers of the box top and bottom.

5 With tassel tied to cord and using a long needle, string cord through center of box so tassel hangs at the bottom, ending with a loop at top for hanging. Embellish with bands of ribbon as desired.

Breathe new life into old holiday cards by transforming them into oversize tag ornaments. Cut out the card design into the desired shape. Glue it to mat board using a glue stick, adding a border of scrapbook paper between the layers; trim, leaving a narrow border. Affix a grommet to the top of the tag and thread with ribbon.

blooms and bells

Illuminate silk flowers by placing them on a string of Christmas lights. Remove the flowers from the stems, saving the petals and plastic fasteners. Discard the stems and leaves. Push an artificial flower onto each of the lightbulbs, securing the plastic fasteners saved from the artificial flowers. Tie bows with 26-inch lengths of plaid ribbon. Using floral wire, secure the bows and jingle bells onto as many bulbs as you desire.

festive facets

～ Papier-mâché goes from plain to pretty in minutes. To get the look, paint a six-sided papier-mâché ornament with blue or sage craft paint. Let dry and then dry-brush with silver paint. Let dry. Turn the ornament upside down so the string is at the bottom; tie on a crystal. Clip string tail once crystal is secure. Glue ribbon to the center of each side. Allow one of the ribbons to make a loop on the ornament top for the hanger.

the big picture

Propped on the mantel or hung on a wall,
animated holiday pictures bring the season alive.

reindeer games

A few snips and punches of paper are all it takes to replicate these prancing reindeer. Make the pictures whatever scale you like using the patterns on *page 156*.

page 156

What You'll Need...

- [ ] pencil
- [ ] tracing paper
- [ ] scissors or crafts knife
- [ ] two 12-inch squares of black cardstock
- [ ] two 12-inch squares of white cardstock
- [ ] circle paper punches, large and small
- [ ] snowflake punch
- [ ] French curves
- [ ] three 12-inch squares of blue solid or subtle-patterned scrapbook paper
- [ ] glue stick
- [ ] 11×14-inch cardstock, any color
- [ ] kneaded eraser
- [ ] two 9×12-inch black frames
- [ ] 11×14-inch black frame

1 Trace deer and tree patterns from page 156 onto tracing paper. Cut out and trace onto black paper. Cut out a total of eight deer and one tree using scissors or a crafts knife.

2 Punch out large holes from black and white papers with circle punch. Punch out small holes and snowflakes from white. Set aside.

3 For snowbanks use French curves to draw random curves along the straight edge of white paper. Make the curves at least 2 inches thick at their narrowest point. Cut out with scissors.

4 For the 11×14-inch frame, trim the blue paper to measure 11×12 inches. Use glue stick to attach it to the 11×14-inch piece of cardstock, aligning it at the top and sides. The snowbank will cover the gap at the bottom edge of the paper.

5 Glue the snowbanks at the bottom of the page.

6 Trim the remaining two blue sheets to 9×12 inches.

7 Attach the snowbanks to the bottom of these pages. Overlap the pieces to create dimension.

8 To help determine the layouts, lay the three pieces on a work surface and line them up across the bottom. This will help make the design continuous from one frame to the next.

9 Using pencil, lightly freehand draw the path of the reindeer to use as a guide for the black dots.

10 Lay all pieces on the backgrounds to achieve the desired look. Adhere the pieces in place with glue stick. Glue on snowflakes and white dots.

11 Erase any pencil marks with a kneaded eraser. Insert a finished piece into each picture frame.

merry and bright

Grab a brush and beret—you're about to become an artist! Actually these painted canvases are so easy to master, you'll want to make groupings or single canvases as gifts this year!

1 Painting one canvas at a time, apply solid color in the center of the canvas. While the paint is wet, paint the contrasting border color, blending slightly. Paint the sides of the canvas. Repeat for the remaining canvases, using the photograph as a color guide. Let the paint dry.

2 Use silver paint and a small flat paintbrush to paint words in the center of each canvas. If desired, lightly write the words on the canvases before painting. You also can use a computer and printer to generate lettering patterns to trace, if desired. Let dry.

3 Arrange the canvases as shown. Cut a cardboard backing piece that fits behind all of the arranged canvases without showing from the front. Use an awl to poke two hanging holes at the top left and right sides, 4 inches in from the canvas edges. Set the cardboard aside.

4 Hot-glue the edges of the canvases together one at a time, being careful not to apply glue where it will show once the canvases are butted together. Glue on the cardboard backing piece. Let dry.

What You'll Need...

- acrylic paints in lime, apple, pink, red, and silver
- flat paintbrushes in medium and small sizes
- 6×12-inch artist's canvas
- two 6×9-inch artist's canvases
- 10×20-inch artist's canvas
- five 4-inch-square artist's canvas
- 5-inch-square artist's canvas
- large piece of heavy-duty cardboard
- scissors
- awl
- hot-glue gun and glue sticks

stretched to fit

Over the river and through the woods, to the fabric store we go! Choose a bold holiday print with large motifs. Buy stretcher bars in the desired sizes (available in art and crafts stores). Cut the fabric 3 inches larger than the size of the stretcher bars after assembled. Center and wrap the fabric around the edges of the canvas stretcher bars, using a staple gun to secure the fabric to the back of the wood frame. Frame the edge with rows of thumbtacks and ribbons.

What You'll Need...

- [ ] two 24-inch-square plastic ceiling tiles in an ice pattern
- [ ] ruler
- [ ] permanent marker
- [ ] straightedge
- [ ] plastic cutter
- [ ] masking tape
- [ ] snowflake ornaments
- [ ] nylon beading string
- [ ] scissors
- [ ] work surface or heavy cardboard
- [ ] drill and drill bit to match bolt size
- [ ] 4 knob back plates
- [ ] 4 machine bolts to fit back plate—1½ inches long
- [ ] 3 machine bolts ⅜ inch long
- [ ] 6 cap nuts
- [ ] 18 washers to fit bolts
- [ ] 14 machine screw nuts to fit bolts
- [ ] photo
- [ ] photo adhesive
- [ ] cardstock
- [ ] paper trimmer
- [ ] photo adhesive pop-up dots

frosty frame

Who would have guessed this wintry frame started out as an ordinary plastic ceiling tile? Draped with icy snowflakes, the glistening squares make a pretty backdrop for a favorite snow season photograph.

1 On back side of plastic, measure and use a permanent marking pen to mark one 24-inch square and one 15-inch square.

2 On back side of plastic, place a straightedge along two markings and cut a line with plastic cutter along edge until it is cut about ¹⁄₁₆ inch deep. It may help to tape the plastic to the work surface and the straightedge firmly to the plastic to keep it stabilized. Make several repetitive cuts.

3 Carefully bend plastic along scored line, with the cut line facing upward and bending the sides down along the scored line.

4 Position the ornaments as desired. The frame, *left*, has an ornament hanging from each side bolt on the diamond, the two bolts at the very top of the piece, and another hidden bolt positioned behind the photo. The arrangement you create will determine the length of the string used to hang the ornaments. Cut string and tie onto each ornament. Trim string for hanging and set it aside.

5 Position the smaller piece of plastic over top of the larger piece of plastic, setting on point as a diamond shape or centered as a square. Tape the two layers together firmly.

6 Measure and mark the top panel corners approximately 1 inch in from the edges for attaching the four knob plates. Also mark spots on the back panel where the hanger attaches.

7 Place plastic on a suitable work surface that will withstand a drill. Drill through both layers of plastic. Drill all four holes plus the two holes on top edge for hanging.

8 Remove the tape and mark the back panel where you want to position another bolt and nut to be used for hanging remaining ornament. This hardware will be hidden behind the photograph. Drill the hole.

9 Assemble the pieces as shown in the diagram on *page 155*. Begin with the nut and bolt that is hidden behind photo. Place washer onto bolt, insert through back side of plastic, add washer, then string from ornament, then cap nut. Repeat this process for the top hanging hardware, inserting hanging string as you assemble.

10 For the four knob plates, also begin from the back side of the bottom piece. Place a washer over the bolt first, insert through the hole, add another washer, a nut, then leave some space. Add another nut, the string from the ornament, a washer, then insert through the next hole from the back side of the plastic

Christmas collage

Gather the precious remnants of Christmases past to display in a glassless gilded frame. A black felt background gives the memorabilia all the attention. Simply hot-glue the items in place and cherish the memories.

Picture This

- [ ] ornaments
- [ ] records
- [ ] record jackets or sleeves
- [ ] sheet music
- [ ] holiday picks
- [ ] photographs
- [ ] snippets of holiday fabrics
- [ ] gift tags
- [ ] tree toppers
- [ ] small boxes wrapped in vintage gift wrap
- [ ] letters to Santa
- [ ] pieces of garland
- [ ] unused holiday napkins
- [ ] place cards
- [ ] greeting cards
- [ ] postcards

top piece. Finish with a cap nut. Adjust the bottom nut downward to fit snugly and adjust the top nut upward to fit snugly. Repeat until all hardware is attached.

1 Decide on the size of the photo to fit in the center of the frame. To prepare the photo, trim it to the desired size. Use photo adhesive or scrapbook adhesive tabs to adhere it to heavy cardstock and trim, leaving a narrow border. If desired, use one or more colors of cardstock to mat the photo. Use adhesive dots to adhere the photo in the center of the plastic frame.

majestic blue and gold

Take your cue from the colors already on your walls and furniture to guide your holiday decorating. Here vibrant blue and rich gold tones blend to make a royal combination.

simple touches

No need to upset the apple cart. Tuck in a few coordinating ball ornaments and sprigs of evergreen to lend a festive touch to existing shelf arrangements.

picture-perfect

A fresh wreath in the window and tree trims on the table make a cozy holiday vignette that's both subtle and sophisticated.

dripping in gold

Gilded ornaments in all shapes and sizes blanket a tree in elegance. Simple matte balls in blue add sparks of color throughout.

45

fit for a king

A simple ribbon. A snippet of evergreen. A gold beaded place mat. The little details will make your dinner guests feel like you've fussed for hours.

encore, encore

    Place a second Christmas tree in an unexpected room of the house, such as a sunporch or guest room. Feel free to shift the style of the ornaments to something more casual while maintaining the cool blue color scheme.

wrapped in color

    Use your theme colors to wrap gifts. If you can't find holiday prints to coordinate, choose everyday wraps that work with your tree. For extra wow top the packages with generous ribbon bows.

47

▶**Your Serve** When company's on the way, you can make serving pieces in seconds. Use large glue dots to marry candleholders and tins. Just be sure to use plenty of dots and keep things centered for stability.

In a Twinkling
decorations

48

◀**String It On** Let decorative tin lids dance their way across a chunky garland. Use a drill or nail and hammer to make holes for stringing. Thread heavy wire through the holes, spacing with large jingle bells.

Let it Snow!

▼ **The Base of It All** Nest a small artificial tree in a holiday tin for a grand alternative to a skirt. Fill the tin to the brim with beaded garland for extra sparkle.

▲ **Lid It Up, Up, Up** Wedge a block of plastic foam into a tin base and poke a ⅛-inch-diameter dowel in the center. Use tin lids with holes drilled in the centers to build a tabletop tree. Use ⁵⁄₃₂ finishing washers to coat the dowel with whimsical ribs of silver and act as spacers between the lids.

◄ **All Aglow** Slip a candle into a tin and melt away the worry of dripping wax. Carry out the colors and design of the tin by surrounding it with small items, such as nuts, fruit, ornaments, and holiday candies.

Note: For safety reasons, never leave burning candles unattended.

words of joy

Sprinkle your home with holiday messages that sing with sentiment. Each of these projects is adaptable for other words and phrases, so you can choose your own favorite sayings to share.

o night divine

 Painted in metallic tones, a variety of lettering provides a whimsical look. A splattering of silver paint in the background appears as tiny stars.

What You'll Need...

- [ ] wood plaque or board
- [ ] black acrylic paint
- [ ] flat paintbrush
- [ ] acrylic metallic paints in gold, silver, blue, pink, copper, green, purple, orange, and red
- [ ] wood stars: 6 small, 3 medium, and 1 large
- [ ] wood glue
- [ ] wood letters to spell desired phrase
- [ ] wood disks or balls with a flat side for "O"s and dots over "I"s, if desired
- [ ] 2 large eye hooks
- [ ] 1½-inch-wide sheer ribbon

1 Paint the wood plaque black. Paint the stars metallic gold. Let the paint dry.

2 Use wood glue to adhere the letters and stars to the plaque. Let the glue dry.

3 Using small amounts of metallic paint on the brush, paint one letter at a time, using a different color for each. When painting barely touch the surface of the wood using diagonal strokes. Let dry. Highlight the letters with silver, brushing in the opposite direction. Let dry. If desired, shadow each letter with a contrasting color, painting in the same manner. Let dry.

4 Dip paintbrush into a little silver paint. Run a finger across the bristles to splatter small dots of paint onto the plaque. Let dry.

5 Screw an eye hook into each end of the plaque on the top. Thread ribbon lengths through each eye hook to hang.

worldly wishes

Make a bold statement with large letters from scrapbooking and crafts stores. Trace around each letter onto patterned paper, cut out, and use decoupage medium to adhere the papers in place. A thin layer of decoupage medium sprinkled with glitter allows the letters to glisten.

say it like it is

One trip to the scrapbooking store and you can make garlands by the dozens. Cut out circles using cutters or punches large enough to hold alphabet stickers. Insert pretty eyelets for hanging and joining letters. Let the merry circles dangle from chain on tiny silver jewelry rings.

mail drop

Wintry white polymer clay graces a greeting card holder with holiday wishes and starry shapes.

1 Prepare clay by kneading and running through a pasta machine on widest setting. Roll out clay to about ⅛ to ³⁄₁₆ inch thick. Continue to run through several times until smooth with an even thickness. Place on smooth, clean work surface where it can be cut.

2 Trace star pattern, *page 156*, onto tracing paper; cut out. Make a pattern for the rectangle to fit your mailbox, if desired.

3 Lay patterns on rolled clay. Use a straightedge and crafts knife to cut around star pattern and rectangle as shown in Photo A, *above*. Cut two stars.

4 Place a small dab of Liquid Sculpey on the center of one star. Turn the second star to alternate points as shown and press down to secure the stars together.

5 Cut out shapes with star cookie cutters. Grommets also can be used to cut out perfect tiny circles. If desired, cut out a star shape from the center of a star using a smaller cutter.

6 Use letters to imprint a message onto a piece of smooth rolled clay.

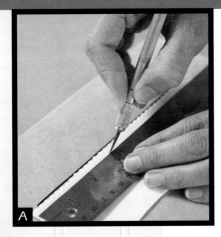

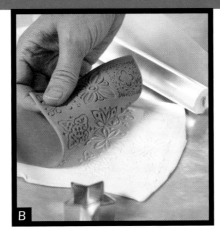

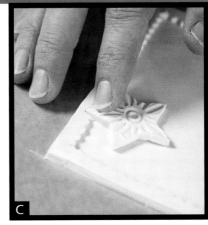

7 Trim around letters to create a banner using a crafts knife. Roll ends inward as on a banner.

8 To create textured stars, place smooth rolled clay onto surface. Place rubber texturizing sheet over clay (texture side down onto clay). Use a roller over sheet to apply even pressure. Roll a few times and remove sheet, leaving impression in clay as shown in Photo B, *above*.

9 Layer and angle other small stars onto each other. You may curve and twist points of stars to make them more interesting. Use a small dab of Liquid Sculpey to adhere one piece of clay to another and press together gently as shown in Photo C.

10 To create borders like the one on the rectangle, roll out clay smoothly and cut a long strip using a pair of decorative scissors. Draw a penciled line onto a piece of paper. Lay the cut piece of clay down on the paper, aligning the cut edge along the line. Lay a straightedge down where you want the straight line to be cut. Trim the clay with a crafts knife. Add a few dots to back of strip of clay and press onto rectangular piece.

11 Cut out small stars for grommets. Leave on work surface and press grommets into clay until they cut through. Place on glass baking dish. Clay is still inside the holes of grommets. Take these stars and the stars that overlap into the border and partially bake them separately before applying them to the rectangular piece. Bake about four minutes at 250°F on a smooth, flat glass baking dish. Let cool. They should be just firm enough to not take a fingerprint when

pressed. Pop out the clay from inside grommets with a crafts knife.

12 Assemble the panel as desired. Add some final textures with different objects such as buttons, a retracted ink pen, phillips screw, crochet hook, etc. Press the partially baked grommeted stars and other stars firmly into the clay. Use a toothpick to clear clay from inside of the grommets. Bake all clay pieces in oven following the clay manufacturer's instructions.

13 Cut a piece of ribbon to desired length. Weave through the bottom star and up into the rectangle panel, allowing the ends of the ribbon to fall behind the clay panel.

14 Spray-paint a wall-mounted mailbox with one first coat of white primer. Let dry.

15 Spray the mailbox with two coats of spray paint in desired color, allowing the paint to dry between coats.

16 Use glitter glue in a fine-tip bottle to draw star designs onto the mailbox. If desired, lay down cookie cutters for patterns and draw around them with glue. Sprinkle with glitter in the same color as the paint. Let dry.

17 Use a generous amount of adhesive to attach the rectangular panel to the front of the mailbox. Let dry.

53

What You'll Need...

- several blocks of white soft polymer clay, such as Sculpey
- pasta machine for clay
- smooth working surface
- tracing paper
- pencil
- scissors
- straightedge
- crafts knife
- Liquid Sculpey
- small star cookie cutters
- small grommets
- imprinting letters for clay
- rubber texturizing sheet
- roller
- decorative-edge scissors
- glass baking dish
- oven
- ribbon
- wall-mounted mailbox
- white spray primer
- spray paint
- glitter glue in fine-tip bottle
- glitter
- strong adhesive, such as E6000

all set for santa

As anticipation mounts, get ready for the jolly ol' elf
with trims, treasures, and treats that celebrate his arrival.

What You'll Need...

- [ ] spray primer
- [ ] wood nesting boxes
- [ ] 3 pieces of pegboard cut to fit the top of each box to serve as lids
- [ ] craft paints in red, green, and gold
- [ ] paintbrush
- [ ] scissors
- [ ] 3 different coordinating decorative 21×29-inch papers
- [ ] decoupage medium
- [ ] wood glue
- [ ] wood ornaments
- [ ] acrylic spray varnish
- [ ] approximately 6 yards of 1½-inch-wide ribbon

stack 'em

Ready to be filled with gifts, these pretty stacking boxes double as storage until St. Nick visits again next year.

1 In a well-ventilated work area, spray all wood pieces with primer. Let dry.

2 Using photo as a guide, paint each box, lid, and wood ornament in red, green, or gold paint. Let dry.

3 Cut corresponding paper for sides and ends of each box. Use decoupage medium to adhere papers to boxes. Add coats of decoupage as desired.

4 Glue wood ornaments onto fronts of papered boxes.

5 Spray acrylic varnish to seal boxes. Let the varnish dry.

6 Secure lid to each box by stringing ribbons through the handle openings and tie bows.

55

good sport

Good girls and boys will love finding Christmas morning surprises tucked in small skates. Double runners work best because they stand all on their own. Replace laces with lengths of holiday ribbon and glue pom-poms or clip hair barrettes to the toe.

sock talk

➳ Wool Christmas stockings trimmed with familiar shapes, beads, and buttons are sure to make Santa smile.

What You'll Need...

for tree stocking

- ☐ tracing paper
- ☐ pencil
- ☐ scissors
- ☐ white wool fabric
- ☐ ½ yard of 45-inch-wide fabric for lining
- ☐ 12×20-inch piece of red wool fabric for cuff
- ☐ fusible webbing; iron
- ☐ 4 different pieces of overdyed green wool fabric at least 6×9 inches
- ☐ 1 scrap of brown overdyed wool fabric
- ☐ matching thread for machine appliqué
- ☐ sewing machine; thread
- ☐ assorted beads; needle
- ☐ 2 yards of purchased white sew-in piping cord

NOTE: Stitch with right sides facing, using ½-inch seams unless otherwise indicated.

TREE STOCKING:

1 Enlarge and trace patterns from pages 154–155; cut out. Use stocking pattern to cut out stocking front and back from white wool.

2 Cut out stocking lining fabric according to pattern. Cut an 11×19-inch piece of red wool fabric for cuff. Cut a 2×5-inch piece of red wool fabric for hanging loop.

3 Trace appliqué tree pattern pieces onto fusible webbing.

4 Using photo as a guide, fuse shapes onto corresponding fabrics. Cut out fabric shapes and fuse to stocking front.

5 With matching threads machine-appliqué the tree, using a close zigzag stitch. Trim with beads as desired.

6 Stitch piping to stocking front along sides and foot. Stitch stocking front to back along piping seam. Trim and clip seam allowance and turn to right side. Stitch lining front and back along sides and foot leaving an opening for turning.

7 With right sides facing, stitch short ends of cuff together. Press cuff in half lengthwise with wrong sides facing and matching the seam. Baste raw edges together and stitch cuff around the top edge of stocking.

57

- tracing paper
- pencil
- scissors
- 1 fat quarter red wool fabric
- assorted contrasting buttons
- ½ yard of 45-inch-wide fabric for lining
- fusible webbing; iron
- several scraps of red and green overdye wool fabric
- matching thread for machine appliqué
- sewing machine
- needle
- 12x20-inch piece white wool fabric for cuff

8 For hanging loop press lengthwise with raw edges in toward the center. Press in half again lengthwise and topstitch along folded edge. Fold loop in half crosswise and baste loop to stocking cuff.

9 Slip stocking into lining with right sides facing and matching the side seams. Stitch around top edge. Trim and clip the seams. Pull stocking through the lining opening. Stitch the lining opening closed.

10 Press lining into the stocking. Keeping cuff free, stitch through lining and stocking around top edge. Turn the cuff down.

STAR STOCKING:

1 For star stocking cut and stitch front to back as for the tree stocking. The star pattern is on *page 154*. For the trim appliqué overdyed wool stars in shades of red and green that have been fused to a white cuff. Sew buttons in their centers.

2 Finish stars with blanket stitches around the edges.

baskets of fun

No mantel? No problem! Deck out a stairway, table, or ladder with cheery baskets lined with personalized fabric napkins. To spruce them up, sew on trim, fringe, ribbon, buttons, and jingle bells, adding a name with self-adhesive scrapbooking letters.

sweet treat

∾ Santa Claus will know exactly which cookie plate holds his treats on Christmas Eve.

What You'll Need...

- paper
- pencil
- 4-inch letter stencil
- tape
- large clear glass platter
- glass paint, such as Liquitex Glossies in white, red, and green; paintbrush
- disposable plate

1 Flip over the letter stencil on paper and trace the *S* and the *C* backward as shown in Photo A, *right.*

2 Tape the pattern to the right side of the glass platter because you will be painting on the bottom side.

3 Use red paint to paint the letters, using the patterns as guides as shown in Photo B. Let the paint dry.

4 Trace holly pattern from *page 157.* Position it near the *C* on the front of the platter and tape in place.

5 On a disposable plate mix a little white into green to soften the color. Paint the holly leaves. Paint the berries red. Let dry.

6 To outline the motifs with dots, dip the handle of the paintbrush into the desired color and dot onto the wrong side of plate as shown in Photo C. To make pink, mix red and white on the plate. For a lighter green, mix just a touch of green into white. Let dry. Flip over the platter and dot its rim with alternating pink and light green. Let dry.

7 Bake platter in oven according to the manufacturer's instructions.

merry mantels

Give your mantel a festive makeover for the holidays.

60

What You'll Need...

- seven 2-inch clay flowerpots
- acrylic paints in red, brown, and pewter
- paintbrush
- round and diamond red acrylic cabochons in a variety of sizes
- glues, such as GemTack, Hold the Foam, and crafts
- eight 2-inch green plastic foam balls
- seven ¼-inch wooden dowels cut into 8-inch lengths
- light green reindeer moss
- 3 green foam floral cones
- four 2½-inch green plastic foam balls
- crystal brads in a variety of sizes in green, red, and crystal
- red-striped ribbon
- floral wire

topiary boulevard

Perched in pretty red pots, these topiaries seem ready to bow when placed in a straight line along the mantel's edge.

1. Paint the bases of the clay flowerpots with red craft paint. Paint the rim of the flowerpots with pewter craft paint. Let dry.

2. Embellish the rims of the flowerpots by gluing on round and diamond-shape red acrylic cabochons.

3. Cut four of the 2-inch plastic foam balls in half. Glue a half of a 2-inch foam ball into the bottom of each flowerpot. These will serve as the bases for the trees.

4. Paint the wooden dowels brown for the trunk of each tree.

5. Once the paint is dry, press a dowel trunk into the center of each flowerpot base. You may want to secure the trunks into the bases with a dab of foam glue.

6. Glue reindeer moss to the plastic foam floral cones, 2½-inch balls, and the rest of the 2-inch balls.

7. Once the cone and round tree components are completely covered and the glue is dry, slide the cones onto three of the wooden trunks. Slide the 2½-inch balls onto the four remaining trunks. Top the larger balls with the 2-inch balls. You may want to secure the tree components with small dabs of foam glue.

8. Decorate the trees with a variety of crystal brads. Top with decorative ribbon bows by securing them to the tops of the trees with floral wire. Complete the topiaries by adding reindeer moss in the top of each pot to cover the foam base.

sparkling mosaics

Traditional holiday colors sparkle with candlelight bouncing off faceted glass. Mosaic candleholders and ball ornaments lend a variety of scale and shape to the arrangement.

starry, starry night

Group star-shape tree toppers for a magnificent cluster of gold. If the stars have a tendency to tip, use pea-size balls of clear candleholder wax to hold the stars upright.

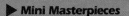

► Mini Masterpieces
Every year several new holiday stamps hit the post office. Use these tiny works of art to craft your next batch of ornaments. Frame the stamps with fancy papers, cutting even borders. Punch a hole at the top and insert a cord for hanging.

In a Twinkling
ornaments

▲ Sand Prints Use dimensional fabric paint to make a design on a matte-finish Christmas ball. Dot on straight from the bottle or brush on with a paintbrush. While the paint is wet, sprinkle with colored crafting sand for velvety texture.

◄ No-Sew Special Glue wedges of textured felt to a circular base for an instant tree skirt. Trim seams with rickrack and edge with pom-pom fringe. No sewing required!

▼ Cookie Cutter So simple to make, yet so pretty to admire, these star-shape ornaments begin with cookie cutters. Drill a tiny hole in one tip and use crafting wire to attach clear plastic beads or baubles that dangle in the center. Top with a ribbon bow.

▲ Impressive Wood Medallions Found in crafts stores, medallions come in several shapes and sizes. Just drill a hole near the top, make a few light brushstrokes of paint, and these patterned beauties are ready for hooks and bows.

◄ Falling Snowflakes Enliven flat leaded-glass ornaments with snowflake stickers. Hang several finished ornaments together to simulate a gentle snowfall.

63

GATHERING *together*

Make the holidays unforgettable by serving your best recipes and sharing unexpected pleasures with family and friends.

65

celebrate
with beaujolais

Combine this wine's fun, festive appeal with some playful French-

nouveau

inspired appetizers for a charming way to gather friends this season.

In late November wine shops often will display jolly, colorful banners exclaiming *"Beaujolais Nouveau est arrivé!"* That means Beaujolais Nouveau has arrived, and it's time to open a few bottles and make merry.

Beaujolais Nouveau may be hard to pronounce (bow-juh-LAY new-VOH), but it's easy to understand and enjoy. *Beaujolais* refers to the French wine-growing region where the wine is produced; *Nouveau* means "new," which refers to its status as a spanking-new wine. Unlike most red wines, which benefit from aging, Beaujolais Nouveau undergoes a special wine-making process that allows it to be enjoyed when very young. The wine is bottled just a few weeks after the grapes are harvested, released in November, and should be consumed within four to 12 months.

69

from France with love

❧ Each November the current vintage of Beaujolais Nouveau arrives in restaurants and wine shops with a flurry of hoopla. The wine is always released on the third Thursday of November—never a minute before. Conveniently that's just in time for holiday celebrations.

This merry and bright red wine is a real crowd-pleaser. Light, fresh, and fruity without the mouth-drying tannins of heavier red wines, it generally pleases both red and white wine drinkers alike—which is to say, it's a great party wine.

While the wine's arrival is a great excuse to gather friends this season, you also can use the libation as a backdrop for any holiday party. Here you'll find a menu of clever takes on French-inspired foods. Each festive bite was chosen especially for its affinity to this wine's food-friendly flavors and playful spirit.

to-go bags

Be sure to have plenty of Beaujolais Nouveau on hand so guests can take a bottle home. Create a quick rustic wrap with a strip of natural burlap stapled at the sides. Corks dangling from twine and snippets of ivy make the take-away extra special.

what's on the menu

Layered scrapbooking papers make a pretty menu presentation. To hold the card, arrange six similar-size corks in two rows and secure them with copper wire. Thread ribbon through two punched holes at the top of the menu card and tie a bow, then slip the card in the center of the cork stand.

ivy to envy

Rich green ivy topiaries blend right in with holiday decorating. Sprinkle them with cork trims and they're dressed for a party. To make the ornaments, screw an eye hook into the top of each cork and finish with a dainty ribbon bow.

Walnut Tartlets with Onions and Goat Cheese,
Les Petits Hot Dogs, Deviled Eggs à la Dijon

Walnut Tartlets with Onions and Goat Cheese

Walnuts often infuse foods of Burgundy.

- ½ of a 15-ounce package rolled refrigerated unbaked piecrust (1 crust)
- ½ cup thinly sliced onion
- 2 cloves garlic, minced
- 2 tablespoons olive oil
- ⅓ cup chopped walnuts, toasted*
- ¼ cup snipped fresh chives
- 1 egg, beaten
- ⅓ cup whipping cream
- ¼ teaspoon salt
- ⅛ teaspoon ground black pepper
- 2 ounces goat cheese (chèvre), crumbled (⅓ cup)

Preheat oven to 400°F. Let piecrust stand at room temperature 15 minutes. Unroll piecrust. Using a 3¼-inch round cookie cutter, cut out nine dough circles (place cutter carefully to cut all circles). Press rounds onto bottoms and up sides of nine 2½-inch tart pans or onto bottoms and partially up sides of nine 2½-inch muffin cups. Prick bottoms with a fork. (If using tart pans, place on a baking sheet.) Bake 5 minutes.

Meanwhile, in a small skillet cook and stir onion and garlic in hot oil until onion is tender and garlic just begins to brown. In a medium bowl combine onion mixture, toasted walnuts, and chives. Divide mixture among tart pans or muffin cups.

In a medium bowl combine egg, whipping cream, salt, and pepper. Add cheese and whisk until nearly smooth. Spoon over onion mixture in tart pans.

Bake 15 minutes or until egg mixture is puffed and set. Let cool in pans on a wire rack for 10 to 15 minutes or until easy to handle. Use the tip of a sharp knife to loosen the pastry from the sides of the pans. Remove tartlets from pans. Serve warm. Makes 9 servings.

*NOTE: To toast nuts, preheat oven to 350°F. Spread nuts in a single layer in a shallow baking pan. Bake for 5 to 10 minutes or until golden brown; watch carefully and stir once or twice.

Les Petits Hot Dogs

These little treats are modeled after French café hot dogs, which often are served smothered with French Gruyère cheese.

- ¼ cup Dijon-style mustard
- ½ teaspoon dried basil, oregano, or Italian seasoning, crushed (optional)
- 1 16-ounce loaf baguette-style French bread, cut into ½-inch slices (about 32) and toasted
- 16 small cooked smoked sausage links, halved lengthwise
- 8 ounces shredded French Gruyère cheese or Swiss cheese (2 cups)

Preheat oven to 375°F. In a small bowl combine mustard and basil (if using). Lightly spread ½ teaspoon mustard mixture on each toasted bread slice. Place slices in a single layer on ungreased baking sheet(s). Top each slice with a smoked sausage link half and about 1 tablespoon cheese. Bake for 5 to 6 minutes or until cheese melts. Serve immediately. Makes 32 appetizers.

Deviled Eggs à la Dijon

Foods and wines from the same region often go well with each other. Both Dijon mustard and Beaujolais Nouveau wine hail from Burgundy, France, so it figures these bites would go well with the wine.

- 8 eggs
- 2 tablespoons Dijon-style mustard
- 2 tablespoons mayonnaise
- 1 tablespoon snipped fresh parsley or 1 teaspoon dried parsley, crushed
- 1 tablespoon snipped fresh tarragon or 1 teaspoon dried tarragon, crushed
- 1 tablespoon snipped fresh chives or 1 teaspoon dried chives
- 1 or 2 cloves garlic, minced
- ⅛ teaspoon salt
  Capers (optional)
  Fresh Italian (flat-leaf) parsley (optional)

In a large saucepan place eggs in a single layer. Add enough cold water to cover the eggs by at least 1 inch. Bring to a rapid boil over high heat (water will have large rapidly breaking bubbles). Remove from heat, cover, and let stand for 15 minutes; drain. Run cold water over the eggs or place them in ice water until cool enough to handle; drain. Peel off eggshells.

Halve eggs lengthwise and remove yolks. Set whites aside. Place yolks in a medium bowl; mash with a fork. Add mustard, mayonnaise, parsley, tarragon, chives, garlic, and salt; mix well. Stuff egg white halves with yolk mixture. Cover and chill until serving time (up to 24 hours). If desired, garnish with capers and/or Italian parsley. Makes 16 appetizers.

Beef Bourguignon Kabobs

Beef Bourguignon Kabobs

These bites are modeled after the famous bistro classic but presented on a party-perfect kabob.

24 6-inch wooden skewers
1 cup Burgundy, Pinot Noir, or other dry red wine
¼ cup olive oil
1½ teaspoons dried thyme, crushed
2 cloves garlic, minced
½ teaspoon salt
¼ teaspoon ground black pepper
12 ounces beef tenderloin steak or beef top loin steak, cut into 1-inch cubes
12 slices bacon, halved crosswise
½ of a 16-ounce package frozen pearl onions (about 1½ cups), thawed
12 fresh mushrooms, halved

Soak wooden skewers in water for at least 30 minutes. Drain.

For marinade, in a small bowl combine wine, olive oil, thyme, garlic, salt, and pepper. Place beef cubes in a large resealable plastic bag set in a shallow dish. Pour marinade over beef. Seal bag. Marinate in refrigerator for 30 minutes.

In a 12-inch skillet cook bacon just until fat begins to render but bacon is still soft. Preheat broiler. Remove meat from marinade; reserve marinade. On each of the skewers alternately thread a piece of beef, onion, mushroom half, and a piece of bacon, weaving the bacon between the other pieces, accordion-style, leaving a ¼-inch space between pieces. Place skewers on the unheated rack of a broiler pan. Brush with reserved marinade.

Broil kabobs 4 to 6 inches from the heat for 6 minutes; turn and brush again with reserved marinade (discard remaining marinade). Broil 6 to 8 minutes more for medium doneness (160°F). Makes 24 kabobs.

Bels Petits Parfaits

Cassis, or black currant, is a popular flavoring in French sorbets, and this easy mini dessert will serve as a refreshing finish to the spread. If you can't purchase cassis sorbet, you can substitute raspberry sorbet or make your own. Hint: Sometimes meringue cookies are located in the baking section of your supermarket.

8 small scoops French vanilla ice cream (about 1 cup)
1 cup crushed purchased meringue cookies (about 18 cookies)
8 small scoops raspberry sorbet or Cassis Sorbet (about 1 cup)
⅓ cup dark crème de cacao
8 fresh mint sprigs

Place a scoop of the vanilla ice cream in each of 8 miniature parfait or demitasse cups. Top each with 1 tablespoon crushed cookies. Top each with a scoop of sorbet, then remaining cookies. Spoon 2 teaspoons crème de cacao over each. Cover and freeze up to 8 hours. Garnish each with a mint sprig. Makes 8 servings.

CASSIS SORBET: In a medium saucepan combine 1 cup water and ¼ cup sugar. Stir over medium-high heat about 5 minutes or until sugar is dissolved and mixture comes to a boil. Add one 12-ounce package frozen unsweetened blackberries and return to a boil; reduce heat. Simmer, uncovered, for 2 minutes, stirring constantly. Press mixture through a fine-mesh sieve into a bowl; discard seeds. Stir in ½ cup black currant syrup or blackberry syrup and 1 tablespoon lemon juice. Pour mixture into a 13×9×2-inch baking pan. Cover and freeze about 4 hours or until nearly frozen. Break frozen mixture into chunks. Transfer to a large chilled mixing bowl. Beat with an electric mixer on medium speed until smooth but not melted. Return quickly to the cold pan. Cover and freeze overnight or until sorbet is firm. Makes 3 cups sorbet.

Smoked Salmon Spread

Smoked salmon is a traditional holiday treat in France, and Beaujolais Nouveau goes beautifully with it.

1 8-ounce tub cream cheese spread with chive and onion
½ cup mayonnaise
1 tablespoon good quality horseradish mustard
4 ounces smoked salmon (not lox-style), flaked, with skin and bones removed
Snipped fresh chives (optional)
Crackers, toasted baguette slices, or desired dippers

In a food processor combine cream cheese spread, mayonnaise, and mustard. Cover and process until combined. (Or beat together in a mixing bowl with an electric mixer until combined.) Transfer to a bowl. Fold in salmon. If desired, garnish with fresh chives. Serve at once with crackers, toasted baguette slices, or dippers. Or cover and refrigerate the spread for up to 3 days; let stand 30 minutes before serving. Makes 1¾ cups spread.

tailored
in toile

Toile in reds and yellows blankets holiday decor with formal flair and pretty pattern. Wide solid ribbons anchor the delightful prints.

Traditional and Timeless

Toile is a symbol of French decorative ingenuity and panache. Created by a German fabric printer in Jouy-en-Josas, France, around 1770, toile departed from the time's typical patterns, such as rococo curves and flamboyant flourishes. Named for its birth city outside of Paris, the fabric became known as toile de Jouy (pronounced twall-de-jhwee), meaning "cloth of Jouy."

   Paired here with satin ribbon, tassels, and hints of gold and silver, the timeless fabric takes on a formal look for the season.

pretty setting

〰 Finish the edges on small pieces of toile to make napkins for everyone gathering around the holiday table. Wrapped with ribbon and topped with a berry sprig, this place setting will be one to remember.

grand gifts

〰 To keep the theme cohesive, wrap Christmas presents in toile fabric and metallic gold. Tie the presents with ribbon or attach pretty tassels to the lids.

hints of red

Bring out the red in the fabric by sprinkling the color throughout the room with accents such as ribbons, berries, and tassels. A cranberry-filled vase and tray give the arrangement an unexpected burst of texture and color.

simply stated

Drape a mantel with greenery to bring the outdoors in. Weave in a single wide toile ribbon and the combination makes a lovely backdrop to showcase coordinating ornaments and small packages.

guest room merriment

Overnight guests will love retreating to a cozy room touched with holiday cheer. No need to go overboard—just an embellished blanket here or a throw pillow there shares love and kindness.

warm and woolly

What You'll Need...

- purchased wool throw
- 2 yards each of 6 different novelty ribbons in various widths (⅜-inch, ½-inch, ⅝-inch, ¾-inch and 1-inch) in red, green, and cream
- 6x60-inch strip of lightweight fusible interfacing
- sewing machine; thread
- sewing needle; scissors
- assorted #3 and #5 perle cotton and embroidery floss in red, green, and cream
- assorted beads for embellishment

Guests can ward off winter's chill with a handsome wool throw. The flower-on-stripe-on-plaid design can be adjusted as desired to fit the colors and widths of your trims. **NOTE:** Fusible webbing on the wrong side of the throw provides stability for ribbons and embroidery stitches.

1 Plan ribbon placement about 6 inches up from the bottom edge of throw.

2 On wrong side of throw, fuse the interfacing 6 inches up from the bottom edge, trimming ends of interfacing.

3 Topstitch ribbons in place to secure.

4 Embellish ribbons and spacing with various embroidery stitches in perle cotton, embroidery floss, and beads, referring to the stitch diagrams on *page 158.*

life's little necessities

Treat guests like royalty with soap, lotion, bath salts, or other pampering products resting next to the sink in a delightful personalized box. Simply paint a papier-mâché box in a festive color and trim with grosgrain ribbon and a sentimental computer-generated message. Enliven the presentation with a glistening snowflake, ball ornaments, and sheer ribbons.

merry mittens

Little ones coming to stay? Make them feel special by placing mini mittens on their pillows. Trim the hand warmers by hot-gluing pom-poms and ribbon bows on the fronts. Buy the mittens to fit, and your little visitors can wear them while building a snowman or taking short winter walks. Place them on top of a book to settle down with at bedtime and tuck in a few sweets to enjoy on the trip home.

82

What You'll Need...

- sewing machine
- thread
- 1½ yards of maxi rickrack for edge
- standard red pillowcase
- 1½ yards each of 5 different medium to jumbo rickracks in green, white, and red
- embroidery floss in assorted shades of red, white, and green
- sewing needle

winter's nap pillowcase

Pretty embroidery floss stitches highlight rows of rickrack in traditional holiday hues.

1 Machine-stitch maxi rickrack along the bottom edge of the pillowcase so that one half of the rickrack shows. Space the five other rickracks 1 inch apart and baste around the pillowcase.

2 Embroider rickrack with shades of floss using lazy daisy, French knots, reverse herringbone, zigzag, and chain stitches referring to the photo as a guide. See *page 158* for stitch diagrams.

jingle all the way

Silk scarves in holiday prints wrap throw pillows with instant holiday magic. Display the pillow on a guest room bed or chair for your visitors to enjoy.

1 Wrap silk scarves around the pillow to resemble a Christmas package, crossing the scarves at the center.

2 Tie the scarf ends together in the front of the pillow, arranging into a bow shape.

3 Hand-stitch, if desired, to secure the scarves to the pillow and hold the bow in place. Use red satin ribbon to tie large red jingle bells to the center of the bow. Knot the ribbon ends and trim with scissors.

What You'll Need...
- purchased green silk square pillow, approximately 20 inches square
- 2 rectangular silk scarves in reds and greens, each approximately 11x54 inches
- matching needle and thread
- red satin ribbon
- 3 large red jingle bells
- scissors

83

White Bean Spread with Fried Sage Leaves and Ciabatta, recipe on page 98

84

Taking full advantage of two of northern Italy's most time-honored ingredients—Prosciutto di Parma and Parmigiano-Reggiano cheese—this easy brunch offers a festive, flavor-charged way to make merry this season. *Buon appetito!*

Italian-inspired

easy does it

As weekend nights become overbooked throughout the holidays, your friends will appreciate it when you say, "Come for brunch." Happily for you, brunch is one of the easiest meals to make.

The recipes here combine some quintessential Italian ingredients and flavor accents, including pine nuts, balsamic vinegar, white beans, Italian flat-leaf parsley, Broccolini, and sage. The true stars of this menu are Prosciutto di Parma—Italy's famous air-cured ham—and Parmigiano-Reggiano cheese.

In much the same way that true Champagne is linked to a place you can point to on a map (the Champagne region in France), Prosciutto di Parma and Parmigiano-Reggiano are linked to a very special place in the world: the northern Italian region of Parma and nearby areas. Both products have been made for centuries in the gently rolling countryside that surrounds the gracious, refined city of Parma. Like Champagne, these products are made using strictly controlled, time-honored methods.

The holidays are a good time to treat yourself and others to these authentic Italian flavors. They'll make your holiday cooking easier and bring both richness and sophistication to the table with very little effort.

Parmigiano-Reggiano Cheese

Renowned cheese expert Steven Jenkins, author of the *Cheese Primer*, calls Parmigiano-Reggiano *"il formaggio migliore nel mondo"*—the world's greatest cheese. What makes it so special? A few answers:

▪ Parmigiano-Reggiano ages for an average of 24 months—the longest of any hard cheese. As it ages it develops a grainy, slightly crunchy texture that's a hallmark of this cheese.

▪ The flavor of Parmigiano-Reggiano can best be described as powerful. A little of this rich, fruity, snappy, and bold cheese goes a long way in cooking.

▪ A number of strict quality controls regulate the making of this cheese; for example, the milk is produced by cows that feed on natural vegetable feed and grasses grown only within a designated region. Authentically produced wheels of this cheese will have the words "Parmigiano-Reggiano" stenciled—in small dots—on the rind. In addition to using it in cooking, serve shards alongside nuts and fruits as an appetizer or a light dessert.

brunch

Broccolini and Italian Cheese Frittata with Prosciutto Crisps

Prosciutto di Parma

To Italians prosciutto simply means "ham," but it is a very different product than American hams. Prosciutto di Parma is salt-cured and air-dried (rather than smoked). Throughout its painstaking curing process, the ham loses more than a quarter of its weight, concentrating its flavors to become sweetly spiced and resulting in a rose-color look with a sheen. For a classic antipasto, Italians often serve very thin slices of Prosciutto di Parma on a platter accompanied by country bread, Italian cheeses, and olives. Here are some other ways to enjoy this delicacy:

- **On Canapés:** Spread thin slices of Italian bread with butter and top with a thin slice or two of Prosciutto di Parma.
- **With Breadsticks:** Butter about an inch of the tips of Italian breadsticks; wrap a thin slice of meat around buttered portion of the breadstick. Serve a half dozen or so in a tall glass.
- **In Salad:** Top vinaigrette-tossed greens with strips of Prosciutto di Parma and shavings of Parmigiano-Reggiano cheese.
- **In Cooking:** Use bits of the meat to flavor soups, sauces, pastas, and meat dishes. Mince thin slices and cook and stir in a little olive oil until crisp, using as you would bacon (though you'll need less prosciutto as it has so much flavor). Cooked prosciutto is also great in scrambled eggs.

Broccolini and Italian Cheese Frittata with Prosciutto Crisps

Served with the frittata, the Prosciutto di Parma takes the place of bacon. Note: For more authenticity and bite, substitute the bitter cousin broccoli raab (also called rapini) for the Broccolini. Buon appetito!

- 1 recipe Prosciutto Crisps
- 1 medium onion, cut into ¼-inch-thick wedges (1 cup)
- 2 cloves garlic, minced
- 2 tablespoons olive oil
- 1 cup sliced, stemmed shiitake mushrooms
- 2 cups chopped Broccolini (stems and florets) or broccoli
- 6 eggs
- ¾ cup freshly grated Parmigiano-Reggiano cheese
- 1½ teaspoons snipped fresh thyme or ½ teaspoon dried thyme, crushed
- ⅛ teaspoon salt
- ⅛ teaspoon ground black pepper

Prepare Prosciutto Crisps; set aside. Reduce oven temperature to 350°F.

In a large ovenproof skillet cook onion and garlic in hot oil until onion is tender, stirring to prevent browning. Add mushrooms and cook until they begin to brown. Add Broccolini; cook and stir for 1 minute or until wilted. Cover and cook about 4 minutes or until crisp-tender. Remove from heat.

In a medium mixing bowl lightly beat eggs. Add ½ cup of the Parmigiano-Reggiano cheese, thyme, salt, and pepper; stir to combine. Pour mixture over vegetables in skillet.

Bake for 12 to 15 minutes or until a knife inserted near the center comes out clean; top with remaining ¼ cup Parmigiano-Reggiano cheese. To serve, loosen frittata with a spatula; cut into wedges. Pile Prosciutto Crisps on top of frittata. Makes 6 servings.

PROSCIUTTO CRISPS: Preheat oven to 400°F. Cut 4 ounces thinly sliced Prosciutto di Parma (about 6 slices) into thin strips. Arrange in a single layer in a 15×10×1-inch baking pan. Bake about 6 to 8 minutes or until fat turns golden and meat darkens slightly; drain on paper towels to crisp.

Roasted Beet, Carrot, And Italian Parsley Salad with Pine Nuts

You'll appreciate the distinctive crunch of pine nuts in this salad.

- 4 medium beets (1 pound)
- 2 tablespoons water
- 3 medium carrots, thinly bias-sliced
- 1 large orange, peeled, sectioned, and coarsely chopped
- 1 recipe Balsamic Vinaigrette
- 1½ cups fresh Italian (flat-leaf) parsley
- ⅓ cup pine nuts, toasted

Roasted Beet, Carrot, and Italian Parsley Salad with Pine Nuts

Preheat oven to 350°F. Place beets on a foil-lined baking sheet and sprinkle with water. Bring up opposite edges of foil around beets. Seal with a double fold. Fold remaining edges to completely enclose the beets, leaving space for steam to build. Bake for 1¼ hours or until beets are tender.

When cool enough to handle, rub off beet skins with a paper towel (use a new paper towel when needed). Transfer beets to a medium bowl. Cover; chill for 2 to 24 hours. Cut into bite-size strips. In a bowl combine beets, carrots, and orange pieces. Pour Balsamic Vinaigrette over beet mixture; toss gently to coat. To serve, arrange parsley on salad plates; top with beet mixture and sprinkle with pine nuts. Makes 6 servings.

BALSAMIC VINAIGRETTE: In a screw-top jar combine 2 tablespoons extra virgin olive oil, 2 tablespoons balsamic vinegar, 1 teaspoon sugar, ½ teaspoon salt, and ¼ teaspoon ground black pepper. Cover; shake to combine.

Pear and Plum Crostata

Winter tarts made with preserved fruits are an Italian holiday tradition.

2 cups all-purpose flour
⅓ cup sugar
1½ teaspoons baking powder
⅛ teaspoon ground cloves
⅓ cup butter
1 egg, lightly beaten
⅓ cup milk
1 teaspoon vanilla
½ cup plum jam
1 tablespoon water or amaretto
1 teaspoon almond extract
4 cups sliced, peeled, and cored
    ripe pears
⅓ cup snipped dried plums
1 recipe Sweetened Whipped
    Cream
    Sliced almonds, toasted
    Thin lemon peel strips

Preheat oven to 375°F. In a medium bowl stir together flour, sugar, baking powder, and cloves. Using a pastry blender, cut in butter until mixture resembles coarse crumbs. In a small bowl combine egg, milk, and vanilla; add egg mixture to flour mixture all at once. Stir just until combined. Shape into ball.

On a lightly floured surface knead dough gently for 10 to 12 strokes or until smooth. With lightly floured hands, pat dough onto the bottom and up the sides of a 10- or 11-inch tart pan with removable bottom. Set aside.

In a small bowl stir together jam, the water, and almond extract until smooth; set aside. Arrange pear slices and plums on dough in tart pan. Spoon jam mixture evenly over fruit. Place tart pan on a baking sheet.

Bake for 35 to 40 minutes or until fruit is tender. If necessary, cover loosely with foil the last 10 to 15 minutes of baking to prevent overbrowning. Cool completely in pan on a wire rack. To serve, remove side of tart pan. Cut into

wedges; transfer to plates. Top with Sweetened Whipped Cream, almonds, and lemon peel. Makes 8 servings.

SWEETENED WHIPPED CREAM: In a medium mixing bowl beat 1 cup whipping cream and 2 tablespoons sugar with an electric mixer on medium to high speed until stiff peaks form.

White Bean Spread With Fried Sage Leaves and Ciabatta

Serve this dip alongside Prosciutto di Parma and a wedge of Parmigiano-Reggiano cheese for authentic northern Italian flavors. Pictured on page 84.

⅓ cup extra virgin olive oil
20 fresh sage leaves
    Salt
1 15-ounce can cannellini beans
    (white kidney beans), rinsed
    and drained
2 tablespoons fresh lemon juice
1 clove garlic, minced
⅛ teaspoon freshly ground
    black pepper
6 slices ciabatta bread, toasted
    and cut into quarters

In a large skillet with straight sides heat oil over medium heat until hot but not smoking. Fry sage leaves about 1 minute until crisp; transfer with a slotted spoon to paper towels. Sprinkle lightly with salt. Reserve cooking oil.

In a food processor or blender combine 3 tablespoons of the reserved cooking oil, beans, lemon juice, garlic, ½ teaspoon salt, and pepper. Cover and process or blend until smooth, scraping down sides of container as necessary. Transfer to a bowl; cover and chill for 2 hours or overnight to develop flavors.

To serve, place bean spread in a bowl. If desired, crumble sage leaves. Sprinkle bean spread with whole or crumbled sage leaves. Lightly brush toasted ciabatta with some of the remaining cooking oil; serve with the spread. Makes 6 servings.

MAKE-AHEAD DIRECTIONS: Prepare sage leaves; cool completely. Store in airtight container at room temperature for up to 2 days. Store toasted bread quarters in an airtight container at room temperature for up to 2 days. Prepare bean spread; refrigerate in an airtight container for up to 2 days.

What to Drink with Brunch

Sparkling wines go better with eggs than just about any other wine, and fortunately Italy sends some beautiful bubblies across the Atlantic. Look for these labels:

▪ **Asti and Moscato d'Asti:** Formerly known as "Asti Spumante," Asti is a fully sparkling wine made from the moscato bianco grape. It's refreshing and fruity, appealing to those who like a little sweetness in their sip. Somewhat similar is Moscato d'Asti, made from the same grape but in a gently sparkling style. For Asti, try the Martini and Rossi label. For Moscato d'Asti, look for Mionetto, Elio Perrone, and Michele Chiarlo.

▪ **Prosecco:** A little less sweet than Asti and Moscato d'Asti, this sparkling wine has a lot going for it: Its fruity, aromatic bouquet makes it easy to love, and it's generally a very good value. Reliable, widely available labels include Zardetto, Martini and Rossi, and Mionetto. For a special occasion, try Santa Margherita Prosecco di Valdobbiadene.

▪ **Franciacorta:** A little higher in image and price, Franciacorta is Italy's answer to French Champagne. Unlike Asti, Moscato d'Asti, and Prosecco, Franciacorta is made using the *méthode champenoise* (that's *metodo tradizionale* or *metodo classico* in Italian). This is the expensive, time-consuming process used to make true French Champagne and results in firmly structured, balanced wines brimming with finesse. Franciacorta is not as widely available as other Italian sparkling wines—ask a local wine merchant who specializes in Italian wines for good recommendations.

88

Pear and Plum Crostata

89

western wonderland

With colors inspired by a vivid Mexican blanket, this holiday decorating scheme is infused with howdy ho-ho-ho. Pair the bright colors with natural tones and textures for an eclectic mix that's both comfortable and exhilarating.

What You'll Need...

- [ ] striped woven Indian blanket 54×74 inches
- [ ] scissors; sewing machine
- [ ] thread
- [ ] sewing needle
- [ ] 6 yards of purchased feather trim
- [ ] 2 yards of leather lacing

feathers all around

Frame the bright blanket stripes with a feathery edge to carry out the Western theme.

1　Cut the blanket into four 27-inch squares.

2　Using the photo as a guide, piece the four squares together so the stripes are turned 90 degrees to each other.

3　Piece squares right sides facing in checkerboard fashion, leaving one seam open to center to allow it to slip around the tree trunk. Cut a 5-inch circle from the center of the piecing.

4　Serge or clean-finish the outside edge of the tree skirt. Turn under ½ inch along clean finished edge of back opening and center circle; topstitch to secure.

5　Stitch feather trim around the outside edge of tree skirt. Tack on leather lacing ties for back closure of tree skirt.

wild west trims

〰 These ornaments are so easy to make, you can craft a set for all your favorite ranch hands. The silver orbs have bands of leather-look trim adhered around the center with crafts glue. Hanging from an earring hoop, the feather trims use an array of inexpensive beads but give the look of real silver and turquoise.

What You'll Need...

- scrap piece of flat plastic foam, such as Styrofoam, or cutting mat
- long and short assorted feathers (available in crafts stores)
- large safety pin
- large round beads in turquoise tones
- decorative plastic silver beads with large holes
- silver earring hoops (available in crafts stores)
- seed beads in assorted colors

1 Lay a feather on the plastic foam or cutting mat. Use the safety pin to poke a hole through the center of the feather, approximately ½ inch from the point.

2 Push turquoise and silver beads onto the feather, leaving the area from the hole to the point free of beads.

3 Thread four seed beads onto the earring hoop in desired pattern. Push the hoop through the hole in the feather. Thread four more seed beads onto the hoop to reflect the bead pattern on the other side of the feather.

4 Tuck a small feather upward into the large beads if desired.

ranch wraps

〰 Faux-leather papers give packages rich texture and color. Conchos, leather-look trims, bright Indian-pattern braid, and jingle bells in coordinating colors will spur gift recipients to shout "Yee-haw!"

What You'll Need...

- assorted ribbons and braids
- scissors
- black grosgrain ribbon
- iron-on hem tape; iron
- cotton woven fabric in natural color
- red leather lacing
- silver concho
- silver beads
- hot-glue gun and glue sticks

93

western pine

Cut in descending lengths, rows of pretty braids and ribbons form a tree shape that bursts with color. With silver bead ornaments and a concho topper, the tree assumes a Western glow.

1 Decide the size of picture desired. The picture, *above*, is 18×24 inches with the longest ribbon 11 inches in length and the shortest 2 inches in length.

2 Alternating ribbons and braids, cut the trims in descending lengths to make a tree shape. Cut a piece of black ribbon for the vertical tree trunk. Cut a piece of hem tape for each ribbon and braid, cutting slightly smaller than the ribbon and braid widths and lengths.

3 Following the hem tape manufacturer's directions, fuse the tree trunk centered vertically on the fabric. Fuse the trim horizontally over the trunk, keeping the pieces evenly spaced.

4 Take the ribbon picture to a professional framer to be matted and framed.

5 Loop a piece of leather lacing through the center bar of the concho. Place a bead on each tail and knot the ends. Trim off the excess lacing. Hot-glue the concho at the treetop and add bead ornaments at the lower edge of the ribbon and braid.

holiday horseplay

Set the stage with a collection of horses on display. Invite colors to the table with a sprinkling of bandannas in green, turquoise, bright pink, and red. Drape them over chair backs and accordion-pleat coordinating cloths cinched with conchos to be used as napkins. Faux-leather papers make fitting place cards nestled in miniature cacti.

leather and lace

Textured faux leather brings a rustic touch to each place setting. Lace one edge with suede that matches the bandanna.

What You'll Need...

- [ ] wavy-edge rotary cutter
- [ ] 13½×18-inch pieces of faux leather fabric
- [ ] eyelets and eyelet tool
- [ ] 1½ yards of suede lacing in a variety of pink, turquoise, red, or green

1 Trim all edges of the place mat with the wavy-edge rotary cutter.

2 Place eyelets along one edge of each place mat, forming two evenly spaced rows. One row of eyelets should be 1 inch from the place mat edge and 1 inch from each other. The other row should be 2 inches from the place mat edge and 1 inch from each other.

3 Lace the suede trim through the eyelets, forming seven cross-stitches.

Easygoing
Appetizer Party

Decadent Dessert Table

Fast and Flexible Family Feast

three beautiful buffets

This year the path to party time is easier than ever with three simple holiday buffets. Team the recipes with decorating ideas to make the gathering dramatic, dynamic, and easy on you.

97

fast and flexible family feast

A holiday dinner in less than two hours?

A little preprep and a quick-cooking pork tenderloin make it so. Here's what makes this feast easy—and flexible.

▪ Big platters on the buffet mean no awkward plates to pass at the table. There is no need to replenish the food as often and no need to keep asking if anyone wants this or that—because diners help themselves.

▪ Serving a Cranberry-Barbecue Sauce will please the kids, while the over-12 crowd will appreciate a sophisticated cranberry chutney. If your family is more about mustard and horseradish, all the easier! Substitute what you like best.

▪ Choose the no-fuss salad and serve on a platter. This allows your family to take exactly what they like (and skip what they don't). Feel free to improvise to make a salad your family

will love; for example, choose apples instead of pears, cheddar instead of blue, walnuts in place of almonds, or your favorite dressings. **Hint:** Kids love ranch dressing—set some out alongside the adult vinaigrette.

▪ Herb Butter Mashed Potatoes are so delightfully creamy and moist.

▪ Looking for a worthy dessert? Borrow one or more from the Decadent Dessert Table, *pages 106–109.*

98

One-Hour Pork Tenderloin with Cranberry Chutney, Green Bean Bake Revisited, Herb Butter Mashed Potatoes, recipes on pages 99–100

Pork Tenderloin with Cranberry Chutney

Few meats offer succulence more simply than a roasted pork tenderloin.

- 3 1- to 1¼-pound pork tenderloins
- 1 tablespoon ground allspice
- 2 to 3 teaspoons cracked black pepper
- 1 teaspoon salt
- 2 tablespoons cooking oil
- 1 tablespoon butter
- 1 large onion, quartered and thinly sliced
- 1 12-ounce package cranberries (3 cups)
- 1 10-ounce jar currant jelly (about 1 cup)
- 1 cup cranberry juice
- ¼ cup packed brown sugar
- 3 tablespoons cider vinegar
- 1 tablespoon grated fresh ginger or ½ teaspoon ground ginger
- ½ teaspoon curry powder
- 2 bunches watercress

Preheat oven to 425°F. Trim fat from tenderloins. In a small bowl combine allspice, pepper, and salt; rub on all sides of tenderloins.*

In a 12-inch skillet brown tenderloins in hot oil over medium heat, turning to brown all sides. Transfer tenderloins to a shallow roasting pan. Roast for 25 minutes or until internal temperature registers 160°F on an instant-read thermometer and juices run clear. Remove from oven and keep warm until ready to serve.

Meanwhile, for cranberry chutney, add butter and onion to the same 12-inch skillet. Cook about 5 minutes or until onion is nearly tender, stirring occasionally. Add cranberries, jelly, cranberry juice, brown sugar, vinegar, ginger, and curry powder to skillet. Bring to boiling; reduce heat. Boil gently but steadily for 20 to 25 minutes or until

thickened to desired consistency and reduced to about 3 cups.

To serve, line a serving platter with watercress. Slice pork and arrange on top of watercress. If desired, spoon some of the cranberry chutney over pork. Serve remaining chutney on the side. Makes 12 to 16 servings.

MAKE-AHEAD DIRECTIONS: Prepare pork and cranberry chutney; allow pork and chutney to cool for 30 minutes. Cover and refrigerate pork for up to 3 days and chutney for up to 1 week. Warm pork in a 350°F oven for 20 to 25 minutes or until heated through. Heat chutney in a saucepan over medium-low heat, stirring occasionally. Serve as above.

*KID-FRIENDLY VERSION: Lightly sprinkle one of the tenderloins with the spice mixture. Continue as directed at left, except serve with Cranberry-Barbecue Sauce instead of the cranberry chutney.

CRANBERRY-BARBECUE SAUCE: In a saucepan combine 1 cup raspberry applesauce, 1 cup bottled barbecue sauce, 1 cup canned whole cranberry sauce, and 2 teaspoons lemon juice. Cook over low heat until heated through, stirring occasionally. Serve with pork.

Green Bean Bake Revisited

Show your family a fresher, more gourmet side of classic green beans.

- 1 large sweet onion (white, yellow, or red), cut into 1-inch wedges
- ¼ cup cooking oil
- 3 tablespoons packed brown sugar
- 2 pounds fresh or frozen whole green beans, trimmed
- 6 ounces baby portobello (cremini) or button mushrooms, halved

- 2 tablespoons olive oil
- 1 tablespoon soy sauce
- 2 teaspoons balsamic vinegar
- 6 ounces goat cheese (chèvre) or cream cheese, softened
- 2 to 3 tablespoons milk

For caramelized onions, in a large skillet cook onion in hot oil, covered, over medium-low heat for 13 to 15 minutes or until tender. Uncover; add brown sugar. Cook and stir over medium-high heat for 3 to 5 minutes or until onion is golden and caramelized. Set aside.

Preheat oven to 400°F. In a large saucepan cook green beans, covered, in a small amount of boiling water for 3 minutes. Drain. In a 3-quart au gratin or baking dish combine green beans and mushrooms. Combine olive oil, soy sauce, and balsamic vinegar. Pour over vegetables, tossing to coat. Roast for 15 to 20 minutes, stirring once, until crisp-tender.

Meanwhile, in a medium mixing bowl beat cheese and milk with an electric mixer on medium speed. Spoon cheese in lengthwise mounds along center of baking dish. Top with caramelized onion. Return to oven; heat for 5 to 8 minutes or until cheese and onion are heated through. Makes 10 to 12 servings.

MAKE-AHEAD DIRECTIONS: Prepare caramelized onion as directed above; cool, transfer to a storage container, and refrigerate until ready to assemble. Prepare beans and mushrooms; cool quickly, transfer to a storage container, and refrigerate until ready to assemble. Remove onion and bean mixture from refrigerator 30 minutes before using. To reheat, return bean mixture to the 3-quart baking dish. Heat in a 400°F oven for 10 minutes. Prepare cheese mixture; spoon over vegetables as directed. Top with caramelized onion. Return to oven and heat for 5 to 8 minutes more or until cheese and onion are heated through.

Herb Butter Mashed Potatoes

Forget last-minute gravy making—there's no need to serve it with these potatoes. Pictured on page 98.

1 recipe Herb Butter, softened
¾ cup half-and-half, light cream, or whole milk
3½ pounds red-skinned potatoes, peeled, if desired, and cut into 2- to 3-inch pieces
1 teaspoon salt

Prepare Herb Butter. Let half-and-half stand at room temperature for 30 minutes. Meanwhile, place potatoes in a 4-quart Dutch oven with enough lightly salted water to cover. Bring to boiling; reduce heat. Cook, covered, for 25 minutes or until very tender.

Drain potatoes. Return to pan with half-and-half, Herb Butter, and salt. Using a large wooden or other sturdy spoon, carefully stir potatoes, smashing lightly by pressing pieces of potato against the side of the pan with the back of the spoon, leaving mixture slightly chunky. Makes about 10 servings.

HERB BUTTER: In a small bowl stir together ½ cup butter, softened; 1 tablespoon snipped fresh Italian (flat-leaf) parsley; 2 teaspoons snipped fresh oregano or ½ teaspoon dried oregano, crushed; 2 teaspoons snipped fresh thyme or ½ teaspoon dried thyme, crushed; and ¼ teaspoon cracked black pepper until combined. Cover and refrigerate at least 3 hours before using to allow flavors to blend. Chill butter for up to 1 week or place in an airtight freezer container and freeze for up to 3 months. Thaw before using. Makes ½ cup.

MAKE-AHEAD DIRECTIONS: Place prepared potatoes in a covered 1½- to 2-quart casserole. Place covered casserole in a 12-inch skillet with 1 inch of simmering water. Hold over very low heat for up to 2 hours.

No-Fuss Blue Cheese and Pear Salad With Apricot Nectar Dressing

No-Fuss Blue Cheese And Pear Salad With Apricot Nectar Dressing

Set out greens and a platter of toppings and let diners create their own salads.

½ cup apricot nectar
⅓ cup extra virgin olive oil
⅓ cup white wine vinegar
1 tablespoon Dijon-style mustard
½ teaspoon salt
3 green onions, finely chopped
½ cup snipped dried apricots
6 ripe red-skinned, Seckel, and/or Bartlett pears, cored and cut into wedges
10 cups mesclun or torn mixed salad greens (about 9 ounces)
½ of a large head radicchio, finely shredded (about 2 cups)
8 to 10 ounces Cambazola or other blue cheese, cut into wedges, or goat cheese (chèvre), cut into rounds
¾ cup slivered almonds, toasted

For dressing, in a very large bowl whisk together apricot nectar, oil, vinegar, mustard, and salt. Stir in green onions and apricots. Add pears to dressing and toss to coat. Cover and refrigerate the pears for 30 minutes to 3½ hours until ready to serve.

When ready to serve, place mesclun and shredded radicchio on a very large serving platter. Use a slotted spoon to remove pear wedges from the dressing; reserve the dressing. Add drained pears and cheese wedges or rounds to platter. Add a small dish of the almonds. Serve the reserved dressing with the salad. Makes 12 servings.

festive fixtures

∾ Generous red ribbon bows add colorful focal points. Ball ornaments grouped in traditional reds, greens, and silver peek out from below the bows.

merry manners

∾ Use fabric glue to make polka-dot napkin rings from felt. Start with 12×4-inch strips and arrange felt circles in the center, making each different, if desired. When the glue starts to set, overlap the ends and glue to secure the strip into a ring.

ring around the evergreen

∾ A circular felt skirt looks lovely at the base of a tabletop tree. Carry through the ball ornament theme with a border of felt circles in shades of green and bright red. Look for premade tree skirts to embellish or cut your own felt circle.

easygoing appetizer party

An after-work get-together, a neighborhood open house, a New Year's Eve spread—this party will work for a variety of occasions throughout the season (and into January, in fact!). The casual bites are adventurous and fun—they'll stir up plenty of conversation. A few pointers:

- Impressive flavors come forth from the two bold and hearty spreads—they serve as the backbone of the buffet.
- Serve the soups in small cups or demitasses that are handy for guests to grab and sip (no spoons needed).

- Round out the buffet with an array of cheese and crackers. For example, Parmigiano-Reggiano will work brilliantly with the bold flavors of the Red Pepper and Artichoke Tapenade.
- If you don't have time to fuss with spreading the Red Onion Marmalade onto toasted baguette slices, simply serve it spread over a log of goat cheese (chèvre) alongside crackers and let guests help themselves.
- If you're hankering for a dessert to serve with this, bake cupcakes frosted with the irresistible frosting from the *White Chocolate Snowdrift Cake, page 109.*

the main man

Give your buffet character—one made of snow! This adorable fellow with an earmuff-to-earmuff grin keeps the mood jolly.

1 Using wood skewers push half of the skewer into a foam ball and the other half into the adjoining ball. Repeat for the remaining foam ball.

2 Cover the snowman figure with batting, molding it to the foam balls. Make wire bobby pins by cutting 4-inch lengths of wire. Fold the wires in half and use the pins to attach batting to the foam balls.

3 Cover the foam ring with batting and set the snowman on top.

4 Cut a ½-inch-wide strip from orange felt. Wrap it around the end of a wood skewer to make a carrot nose shape. Trim the skewer end to approximately 4 inches. Poke the nose into the center of the snowman's face.

5 Use quilting pins to attach the pom-pom eyes to the snowman face. Pin the buttons to the face and down the body.

6 Tie the fleece scarf around the neck. Place the earmuffs on the head and tuck in a sprig of holly. Poke an evergreen arm into each side.

7 Dangle doll skates and felt snowflakes from the branches.

Green Pea Soup

Another time consider serving this great-tasting soup in larger portions as a first course to a sit-down dinner. Pictured on page 104.

    ½ cup chopped onion (1 medium)
    2 tablespoons butter
    2 14-ounce cans reduced-sodium
        chicken broth
    1 16-ounce package frozen baby
        sweet peas
    1 head butterhead lettuce, torn
        (about 4 cups)
    1 tablespoon snipped fresh
        oregano or 1 teaspoon dried
        oregano, crushed
    2 ounces goat cheese (chèvre), or
        2 ounces cream cheese plus
        1 tablespoon lemon juice
        Sea salt or kosher salt
        Freshly ground black pepper

In a 4-quart Dutch oven cook onion in hot butter over medium heat about 5 minutes or until onion is tender, stirring occasionally.

Add chicken broth and peas to onion in Dutch oven. Bring to boiling; reduce heat. Simmer, uncovered, about 5 minutes or until peas are tender. Add

lettuce; cook about 1 minute more or until lettuce is wilted. Remove from heat. Stir in oregano. Cool slightly, about 10 minutes.

Transfer half of the hot pea mixture to a blender or food processor. Cover and blend or process until smooth. Repeat with remaining pea mixture. Return all to Dutch oven. Break apart goat cheese and add to soup. (Or cut up cream cheese and stir into soup with lemon juice.) Heat and whisk until cheese is melted and soup is heated through. Season to taste with salt and pepper. Serve at once in demitasse cups or small heatproof glasses. Makes about 6 cups (eighteen ⅓-cup servings).

MAKE-AHEAD DIRECTIONS:
Prepare soup as directed. Cover and refrigerate for up to 2 days. To serve, in a Dutch oven bring soup to simmering over medium-low heat. Remove from heat; serve immediately.

What You'll Need...

- wood skewers
- two 8-inch plastic foam balls
- 6-inch plastic foam ball
- sheet of polyester quilt batting
- floral wire
- wire cutter
- 10-inch plastic foam ring
- orange felt
- scissors
- quilting pins
- black pom-poms
- small black buttons
- large red buttons
- 6×48-inch piece of red plaid fleece, fringed on short ends
- red earmuffs
- holly sprig
- two 14-inch-long evergreen branches
- doll skates
- 2 felt snowflake ornaments

Red Pepper and
Artichoke Tapenade

15-Minute Zesty
Smoked Trout Spread

Tomato Bisque
Sip Soup

Green Pea Soup,
recipe on page 102

104

Red Onion Marmalade and
Goat Cheese Canapés

15-Minute Zesty Smoked Trout Spread

Keep the ingredients on hand and you'll be just minutes from an appetizer.

- 8 ounces smoked trout fillets (or other smoked whitefish), skin and bones removed and flaked
- 2 3-ounce packages cream cheese, softened
- ¼ cup dairy sour cream
- 3 tablespoons finely chopped shallot or onion
- 1½ teaspoons finely shredded lemon peel
- 3 tablespoons lemon juice
- ¼ teaspoon freshly ground black pepper
- Fresh chives or chopped green onion (optional)
- 3 medium red, green, and/or orange sweet peppers, cut into 1-inch-wide strips
- Assorted crackers or flatbreads

In a bowl stir together smoked trout, cream cheese, sour cream, shallot, lemon peel, lemon juice, and pepper until combined, mashing trout against sides of bowl with back of spoon while stirring.

Transfer spread to a small serving bowl. Cover and refrigerate for 1 hour or up to 24 hours. Remove spread from refrigerator about 15 minutes before serving. If desired, top with chives. Serve with pepper strips and crackers. Makes 1¾ cups spread.

Red Pepper and Artichoke Tapenade

This garlicky dip is bold in flavor.

- 1 15- to 16-ounce jar roasted red sweet peppers, drained
- 2 6-ounce jars marinated artichoke hearts, drained
- ½ cup shredded Parmesan cheese
- ⅓ cup capers, drained
- 2 tablespoons snipped fresh parsley or basil
- 1 tablespoon lemon juice
- 2 to 3 cloves garlic, coarsely chopped
- ½ teaspoon salt
- ¼ teaspoon ground black pepper
- ¼ cup olive oil
- Toasted baguette slices or assorted crackers

In a food processor or blender combine sweet peppers, artichoke hearts, Parmesan cheese, capers, parsley, lemon juice, garlic, salt, and black pepper. Cover and process or blend until combined. With processor or blender running, slowly add oil in a steady stream until mixture is combined and nearly smooth.

Transfer to a serving bowl. Cover and refrigerate for 1 to 6 hours. Serve with baguette slices. Makes 3 cups spread.

MAKE-AHEAD DIRECTIONS: Prepare as above, except do not add parsley or basil. Cover; refrigerate for up to 24 hours. Stir in parsley before serving.

Red Onion Marmalade And Goat Cheese Canapés

This marmalade also tastes divine on creamy mascarpone cheese.

- 2 large red onions, chopped (4 cups)
- 1 cup packed brown sugar
- 1 cup red wine vinegar
- 2 teaspoons snipped fresh thyme or ½ teaspoon dried thyme, crushed
- 4 cloves garlic, minced
- 36 thinly sliced baguette slices, toasted
- 6 ounces soft goat cheese (chèvre)
- Snipped fresh thyme (optional)

For marmalade, in a medium saucepan combine onion, brown sugar, vinegar, dried thyme (if using), and garlic. Bring to boiling over medium heat; reduce heat. Simmer, uncovered, for 45 to 50 minutes or until onion is tender and liquid is nearly evaporated. (Mixture will thicken more as it cools.) Stir in fresh thyme (if using); remove from heat and allow to cool. Use immediately or cover and refrigerate for up to 1 week.

Just before serving spread toasted baguette slices with goat cheese. Spoon some of the marmalade over each. If desired, garnish with snipped fresh thyme. Makes 36 appetizers.

Tomato Bisque Sip Soup

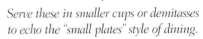

Serve these in smaller cups or demitasses to echo the "small plates" style of dining.

- 3 14½-ounce cans diced tomatoes with garlic and onion, undrained
- 1 tablespoon balsamic vinegar
- 1 tablespoon packed brown sugar
- 1½ teaspoons finely shredded orange peel
- ¼ teaspoon cracked black pepper
- ¾ cup whipping cream
- 1 to 2 ounces Parmesan cheese, shaved (optional)
- Cracked black pepper (optional)

Place two cans of the tomatoes in a blender. Cover; blend until very smooth. Transfer to a large saucepan. Cover; blend remaining tomatoes, vinegar, brown sugar, peel, and ¼ teaspoon pepper until very smooth. Pour into the saucepan. Bring to simmering over medium-low heat. Simmer, uncovered, for 5 minutes; remove from heat.

Stir in whipping cream until combined. Serve at once in demitasse cups or small heatproof glasses. If desired, sprinkle each serving with cheese and additional pepper. Makes about 5½ cups (sixteen ⅓-cup servings).

105

Fluffy Cranberry Mousse, recipe on page 109

Brandied Cherry-Raisin Bars, recipe on page 108

White Chocolate Snowdrift Cake, recipe on page 109

decadent dessert table

This buffet calls on one of the best entertaining strategies of all time: make ahead. Everything can be prepared in advance, with just a few flourishes at the last minute. So head to the holiday symphony, the *Nutcracker* ballet, or the kids' Christmas pageant. Then come home and keep the magic alive. A few tips:

- The star of the buffet is the White Chocolate Snowdrift Cake, and the star of the cake is the frosting. If you're short on time, order an unfrosted cake or cupcakes from the bakery and top with the lavish frosting.

- With food this beautiful, you don't need to decorate much. Use clear glass platters and bowls to show off your creations. To add drama vary the height of the desserts with pedestals.

- Make extra batches of the Brandied Cherry-Raisin Bars and the Good Cheer Holiday Crunch and package them festively for your guests to take home.

Good Cheer Holiday Crunch, recipe on page 108

dessert table

Let the billowy Fluffy Cranberry Mousse and the showy White Chocolate Snowdrift Cake star on your dessert table. Placed against a backdrop of poinsettias and wrapped packages, the buffet will make the room merry and bright—without a lot of work on your part.

evenly. Bake about 40 minutes more or until a wooden toothpick inserted in center comes out clean (if necessary, cover loosely with foil the last 10 minutes of baking to prevent overbrowning). Cool completely in pan on a wire rack. If desired, sprinkle with powdered sugar. Cut into bars. Makes 16 bars.

TO STORE: Place bars in layers separated by waxed paper in an airtight container; cover. Store in the refrigerator for up to 3 days.

Good Cheer Holiday Crunch

For a kid-friendly version, substitute ¼ cup unsweetened cocoa powder for the nutmeg, peanuts for cashews, dried fruit bits for dried cherries, and peanut butter for cashew butter. Pictured on page 107.

  1½ cups powdered sugar
   ½ teaspoon ground nutmeg
   8 cups bite-size corn or rice
       square cereal
   1 cup white baking pieces
   ½ cup cashew butter
   ¼ cup butter, cut up
   ¼ teaspoon vanilla
  1½ cups lightly salted cashews
  1⅓ cups dried cherries or cranberries
       and/or chopped dried apricots
       (about 6 ounces)

In a very large plastic bag combine powdered sugar and nutmeg; set aside. Place cereal in a very large bowl.

In a medium saucepan combine white baking pieces, cashew butter, and butter. Stir over low heat until baking pieces and butter are melted. Remove from heat. Stir in vanilla.

Pour butter mixture over cereal; carefully stir until cereal is evenly coated. Cool slightly. Add cereal mixture, half at a time, to powdered sugar mixture in bag; shake to coat. Add nuts and fruit. Shake just until combined. Pour into shallow baking pan lined with waxed paper to cool. Store in airtight container for up to 2 days. Makes about 14 cups.

take-away tree

 Don't let guests leave empty-handed. Place extra bars and party mix in plastic bags and twist shut with a decorative wire. Put the goodies inside large pull-apart plastic ornaments topped with ribbon bows to offer guests when the party's over.

Brandied Cherry-Raisin Bars

Another time top bars with whipped cream for dessert. Pictured on page 106.

  ¾ cup halved candied cherries
  ½ cup golden raisins
  ½ cup brandy or water
  1 cup all-purpose flour
  ⅓ cup packed brown sugar
  ½ cup butter
  2 eggs
  1 cup packed brown sugar
  ½ cup all-purpose flour
  1 teaspoon vanilla
  ⅓ cup chopped pecans
     Powdered sugar (optional)

In a small saucepan stir together candied cherries, raisins, and brandy; bring to boiling. Remove from heat. Let stand for 20 minutes; drain.

Preheat oven to 350°F. For crust, in a medium bowl stir together 1 cup flour and ⅓ cup brown sugar. Using a pastry blender, cut in butter until mixture resembles coarse crumbs. Press mixture into bottom of an ungreased 8×8×2-inch baking pan. Bake about 20 minutes or until golden.

For topping, in a medium mixing bowl beat eggs with an electric mixer on low speed for 4 minutes; stir in 1 cup brown sugar, ½ cup flour, and vanilla just until combined. Stir in pecans and fruit. Pour topping over baked crust, spreading

White Chocolate Snowdrift Cake

White Chocolate Snowdrift Cake

This dessert starts with a cake mix, but if you're a from-scratch baker, feel free to bake your favorite chocolate or white cake. Either cake flavor will go beautifully with the luscious homemade frosting.

    ¾ cup whipping cream
    8 ounces white baking chocolate,
       chopped
    1 package 2-layer-size white
       cake mix
    ⅓ cup unsweetened cocoa
       powder
    1 8-ounce package cream cheese,
       cut up and softened
    1 cup powdered sugar
       Sugared Rosemary and
       Cranberries (optional)

For frosting, in a medium saucepan combine whipping cream and chocolate. Cook, stirring occasionally, over low heat until chocolate is completely melted and smooth. Transfer to a large mixing bowl; cover and refrigerate until completely chilled, at least 2 hours.

Meanwhile, grease and flour two 9×1½-inch or 8×1½-inch round cake pans; set aside.

Prepare white cake mix according to package directions. Spoon about 1½ cups of the batter into each cake pan. Sift cocoa powder over batter remaining in bowl; stir until combined. Spoon cocoa batter on white cake mix batter in pans. Using a knife or spatula, gently cut through the batters to marble. Bake according to package directions, except check cakes several minutes before minimum time indicated on package.*

Let cakes cool in pans on wire racks for 10 minutes. Remove cakes from pans; cool completely on wire racks.

Add cream cheese to chilled white chocolate mixture; beat with an electric mixer until smooth. Gradually add powdered sugar, beating until the sugar is completely combined. (Mixture should hold soft peaks; do not overbeat.) Use immediately.

Place one cake layer on a serving platter. Frost with about ¾ cup frosting. Top with second cake layer. Frost top and sides of cake.

Serve immediately or cover and refrigerate until serving time (up to 4 hours). If desired, garnish cake with Sugared Rosemary and Cranberries before serving. Makes 12 servings.

SUGARED ROSEMARY AND CRANBERRIES: Lightly spray several rosemary sprigs and cranberries with nonstick cooking spray. Sprinkle granulated sugar on rosemary; roll cranberries in a small amount of granulated sugar to coat. Place on waxed paper for at least 1 hour before using. This is a decorative, not edible, garnish.

***TEST KITCHEN TIP:** The added cocoa powder will make the cakes bake in a shorter time than instructed on the cake package.

Fluffy Cranberry Mousse

Serve this refreshing dessert after a heavy holiday meal. Pictured on page 106.

    ½ an 8-ounce package cream
       cheese, softened
    2 tablespoons sugar
    ½ teaspoon vanilla
    ½ cup frozen cranberry juice
       concentrate, thawed
    1 16-ounce can whole
       cranberry sauce
    1½ cups whipping cream
    1 recipe Sweetened Cranberries

In a large mixing bowl beat cheese with an electric mixer on medium speed for 30 seconds. Beat in sugar and vanilla until smooth. Slowly add cranberry juice concentrate, beating until very smooth. In a small bowl stir cranberry sauce to remove any large lumps; set aside.

In a chilled large mixing bowl beat whipping cream with an electric mixer on low to medium speed until soft peaks form. Fold about half the cranberry sauce and half the whipped cream into the cream cheese mixture until combined. Fold in remaining sauce and cream.

Serve immediately or cover and refrigerate up to 24 hours (if chilled, stir before serving). To serve, spoon into a large serving bowl, 24 chilled demitasse cups, or 12 chilled small dessert dishes. Spoon Sweetened Cranberries on top just before serving. Makes 24 (¼-cup) servings or 12 (½-cup) servings.

SWEETENED CRANBERRIES: In a medium skillet combine 1 cup fresh cranberries, ⅓ cup sugar, and 2 tablespoons water. Cook and stir over medium heat until sugar is dissolved and cranberries just begin to pop. Remove from heat. Cover; chill until serving time.

FROZEN MOUSSE: Prepare mousse as above. Spoon into 12 freezer-safe small dessert dishes. Cover; freeze for 24 hours or until firm. To serve, uncover and let stand for 1 to 2 minutes to soften slightly.

candy cane trees

Gather candy canes, peppermints, and other red and white candies as the ingredients to whip up sweet holiday trees. Hot-glue the pieces onto plastic foam cones using your imagination to guide you.

peppermint pizzazz

There's something playful and familiar about peppermint candies. They remind us of life's simple pleasures. Use red-and-white delights, such as candy canes, peppermint pillows, candy sticks, and more, to add a touch of whimsy to your home this holiday season.

minty fresh

❧ Nestle red-and-white-striped candles in a platter of candy for an unexpected presentation. Be sure to offer a separate bowl of sweets so no one reaches for an after-dinner mint among the burning candles.

come to dinner

❧ Jazz up a place setting faster than Santa can say "and to all a good night" using a translucent red cookie cutter as a party favor. Tuck a candy cane through the cutter's handle, then tie it up with red and white cord and a tiny pinecone-and-berry sprig. Carry out the theme with wide striped ribbon lengths across the table. Clear glass dinnerware anchors the ribbon and lets the candy cane stripes shine through.

Pumpkin Chocolate Cheesecake Bars

beautiful bars

Bar cookies are among the easiest cookies to make—you simply mix, pour, and bake something spectacular. Here are all kinds—from kid friendly to sophisticated. Whether you offer them on a cookie tray or let them star as dessert, they're always holiday hits.

Pumpkin Chocolate Cheesecake Bars

Do you want to feature pumpkin, yet everyone craves chocolate? This bar solves the dilemma!

- 1 recipe Graham Cracker Crust
- 2 8-ounce packages cream cheese, softened
- 1¾ cups sugar
- 3 eggs
- 1 cup canned pumpkin
- ½ teaspoon pumpkin pie spice
- ½ teaspoon vanilla
- ¼ teaspoon salt
- 6 ounces semisweet chocolate, cut up, or 1 cup semisweet chocolate pieces
- 2 tablespoons butter
- 1¼ cups dairy sour cream
- ¼ cup sugar
- Grated fresh nutmeg

Preheat oven to 325°F. Prepare Graham Cracker Crust; set aside.

In a large mixing bowl beat cream cheese and 1¾ cups sugar with an electric mixer on medium speed until smooth. Add eggs, 1 at a time, beating on low speed after each addition just until combined. Beat in pumpkin, spice, vanilla, and salt on low speed just until combined. Pour 1¼ cups of the filling into a bowl. Set both bowls aside.

In a small heavy saucepan heat chocolate and butter over low heat until melted, stirring frequently. Whisk the melted chocolate mixture into the 1¼ cups filling. Carefully spread the chocolate filling evenly over Graham Cracker Crust. Bake for 15 minutes. Remove from oven. Carefully pour remaining pumpkin filling over baked chocolate layer, spreading evenly.

Bake for 40 to 45 minutes more or until mixture is puffed and center is set. Cool in pan on a wire rack for 30 minutes. Meanwhile, combine sour cream and ¼ cup sugar. Cover; let stand at room temperature while bars cool. Gently spread the sour cream mixture over bars. Cool completely. Cover and refrigerate for 3 to 24 hours before cutting. Sprinkle with nutmeg just before serving. Cut into bars or triangles.* Makes 24 to 36 bars.

GRAHAM CRACKER CRUST: Lightly grease a 13×9×2-inch baking pan. In a medium bowl combine 1¼ cups graham cracker crumbs and ¼ cup sugar. Add ⅓ cup melted butter; mix well. Press evenly into the bottom of prepared pan.

*NOTE: To make cutting easier, line the baking pan with foil and grease the foil before pressing the graham cracker crust into the pan. To cut into triangles, make three crosswise cuts in the chilled bars, dividing pan into four equal strips. Cut five triangular-shape pieces from each strip plus two end half-triangles. Repeat with remaining strips.

TO STORE: Place bars in a single layer in an airtight container; cover. Store in refrigerator up to 3 days. Do not freeze.

Cherry and Chocolate Chunk Brownies

Enjoy two favorite flavors in one bar.

- 1 cup butter
- 6 ounces unsweetened chocolate, coarsely chopped
- 2 cups sugar
- 4 eggs
- 2 teaspoons vanilla
- 1⅓ cups all-purpose flour
- ½ teaspoon baking soda
- ¼ teaspoon salt
- ¼ teaspoon ground cardamom
- 1 cup dried tart cherries
- 2 ounces bittersweet or semisweet chocolate, chopped
- Powdered sugar (optional)

Preheat oven to 350°F. In a large saucepan melt butter and unsweetened chocolate over low heat, stirring constantly. Remove saucepan from the heat; cool.

Grease a 13×9×2-inch baking pan; set aside. Stir sugar into cooled chocolate mixture in saucepan. Add eggs, 1 at a time, beating with a wooden spoon after each addition just until combined. Stir in vanilla.

In a medium bowl combine flour, baking soda, salt, and cardamom. Add flour mixture to chocolate mixture; stir just until combined. Stir in cherries and bittersweet chocolate. Spread batter in prepared pan.

Bake for 30 minutes. Cool in pan on a wire rack. Cut into bars. If desired, decorate cut bars by placing stencils on top and dusting with powdered sugar. Makes 24 bars.

TO STORE: Place brownies in layers separated by waxed paper in an airtight container; cover. Store at room temperature for up to 2 days or freeze for up to 3 months.

Cherry and Chocolate Chunk Brownies

Deep Chocolate Brownies

Five-Layer Bars

Deep Chocolate Brownies

For some people, only the deepest, richest, chocolatiest bars will do.

　1　egg
　1　cup butterscotch-flavor
　　　ice cream topping
　2　cups coarsely chopped pecans
　2　cups flaked coconut
　¾　cup butter, softened
1½　cups packed dark brown sugar
　8　ounces bittersweet chocolate,
　　　melted and cooled
　2　eggs
　2　teaspoons vanilla
　2　cups all-purpose flour
　1　teaspoon baking powder
　½　teaspoon baking soda
　½　teaspoon salt
　1　12-ounce package semisweet
　　　chocolate pieces (2 cups)

Preheat oven to 350°F. Lightly grease a 13×9×2-inch baking pan; set the pan aside.

For nut mixture, in a medium mixing bowl beat 1 egg with an electric mixer on medium speed until fluffy and light colored. Stir in ice cream topping. Fold in pecans and coconut; set aside.

In a large mixing bowl beat butter with an electric mixer on medium to high speed for 30 seconds. Beat in brown sugar until combined. Beat in

cooled bittersweet chocolate, 2 eggs, and vanilla. Stir together flour, baking powder, baking soda, and salt; stir into chocolate mixture. Stir in chocolate pieces. Spread the batter in prepared pan; spread nut mixture over batter.

Bake about 35 minutes or until golden and set. Cool in pan on a wire rack. Cut into bars. Makes 24 bars.
TO STORE: Place brownies in a single layer in an airtight container; cover. Store at room temperature for up to 2 days.

Five-Layer Bars

These nicely nutty bars are so much easier to make than they look!

　2　13-ounce packages soft coconut
　　　macaroon cookies (32 cookies)
　¾　cup sweetened condensed milk
　¾　cup semisweet chocolate pieces
　¾　cup raisins, dried cranberries, or
　　　golden raisins and
　　　dried cherries
　1　cup coarsely chopped peanuts

Preheat oven to 350°F. Arrange cookies in the bottom of a greased 13×9×2-inch baking pan. Press cookies together to form a crust. Bake for 12 minutes.

Remove from oven. Drizzle crust evenly with condensed milk. Sprinkle with chocolate pieces, raisins, and

peanuts. Bake for 25 minutes or until edges are lightly browned. Cool in pan on a wire rack. Cut into bars. Makes 30.
TO STORE: Place bars in a single layer in an airtight container; cover. Store at room temperature for up to 3 days.

Key Lime Cheesecake Bars

Count on these pretzel-crusted bars, topped with fresh lime and pistachios, to add a little zing to a cookie tray.

2½　cups pretzel sticks, finely crushed
　　　(1 cup)
　2　tablespoons sugar
　½　cup butter, melted
　2　8-ounce packages cream cheese,
　　　softened
　⅔　cup sugar
　1　teaspoon vanilla
　3　eggs
1½　teaspoons finely shredded
　　　lime peel
　3　tablespoons bottled key lime
　　　juice or regular lime juice
　¼　cup chopped salted
　　　pistachio nuts
　　　Lime slices (optional)

Preheat oven to 350°F. Grease the bottom of a 2-quart rectangular baking dish; set aside.

For crust, in a medium bowl stir together crushed pretzels, 2 tablespoons

114

Key Lime Cheesecake Bars

Peanut Butter Bars

sugar, and melted butter. Press pretzel mixture evenly into bottom of the prepared baking dish. Bake for 10 minutes; cool on a wire rack while preparing filling.

For filling, in a large mixing bowl beat cream cheese, ⅔ cup sugar, and vanilla with an electric mixer on medium to high speed until combined. Add eggs all at once. Beat on low speed just until combined. Stir in lime peel and lime juice. Pour cream cheese mixture over crust. Sprinkle with pistachio nuts.

Bake for 20 to 25 minutes or until center appears set. Cool in baking dish on a wire rack for 30 minutes. Cover; refrigerate for 4 to 24 hours (top will crack slightly). If desired, garnish bars with lime slices. Makes 15 to 20 bars.

TO STORE: Place bars in a single layer in an airtight container; cover. Store in the refrigerator for up to 3 days. Do not freeze the bars.

Peanut Butter Bars

For families with kids, sometimes simplest is best! Dried cranberries add a seasonal angle to these bars.

½ cup dried cranberries
¼ cup boiling water
¼ cup butter, softened
½ cup chunky peanut butter*

⅓ cup packed brown sugar
1 cup all-purpose flour
½ cup finely chopped peanuts
2 3-ounce packages cream cheese, softened
¼ cup granulated sugar
1 egg
⅔ cup chunky peanut butter*
1 tablespoon lemon juice

Preheat oven to 350°F. Grease an 8×8×2-inch baking pan; set aside. In a small bowl combine cranberries and boiling water. Cover and let stand for 20 minutes. Drain well.

In a large mixing bowl beat butter and ½ cup peanut butter with an electric mixer until combined. Beat in the brown sugar. Beat in the flour on low speed (mixture will be crumbly). Stir in the peanuts and drained cranberries. Reserve 1 cup of the crumb mixture.

Press remaining crumb mixture into bottom of the prepared pan. Bake for 12 minutes.

Meanwhile, for filling, in a medium bowl beat the cream cheese and granulated sugar with an electric mixer until smooth. Add egg, ⅔ cup peanut butter, and lemon juice; beat until combined. Spread evenly over crust. Sprinkle reserved crumb mixture over top, lightly pressing into filling.

Bake about 25 minutes more or until top is lightly browned and edges are puffed. Cool in pan on a wire rack. Cut into bars. Makes 16 bars.

***NOTE:** Do not use natural peanut butter in this recipe.

TO STORE: Place bars in a single layer in an airtight container; cover. Store in the refrigerator for up to 2 days.

Tips for Great Bar Cookies

▪ **Be sure to use the right pan** for the job. Select a metal baking pan for the fastest, most even baking and always use the pan size the recipe suggests. Too large a pan yields bars that are too thin, while too small a pan leaves bars too thick to cook evenly.

▪ **To cut bars into triangles,** slice into 2- or 2½-inch squares. Cut each square in half diagonally. Or cut bars into rectangles and cut each diagonally into triangles.

▪ **To make diamonds,** cut parallel lines 1 or 1½ inches apart down the length of the pan. Then cut diagonal lines the same distance apart across the pan, forming diamond-shape bars.

▪ **To add a stenciled design to unfrosted bars,** lay waxed paper strips across the top in a pattern. Sprinkle with a mixture of powdered sugar and a spice from the recipe or use a mixture of powdered sugar and cocoa powder.

▪ **To decorate frosted bars,** sprinkle with grated chocolate or chocolate curls, miniature chocolate chips, chopped nuts, or dried or candied fruit.

Celebrate
Hanukkah with
the Star of David
leading the way.
These projects use
the same pattern in
two different ways
to create a glistening
candle and greetings
of joy.

star light, star bright

studded star

Using a photocopy of the pattern on *page 155*, you can make this candle in minutes. Place the pattern over the candle and use an upholstery tack to poke through the paper at each pattern dot. Remove the pattern and push in an upholstery tack at each mark.

Note: For safety reasons, never leave burning candles unattended.

wrapped in gold

Layer pretty papers, metallic blue brads, and golden embroidery floss to make this greeting card a keeper.

What You'll Need...

- [ ] photocopier
- [ ] 5⅞x11¾-inch piece of white cardstock
- [ ] 5-inch square of metallic gold paper
- [ ] 4½-inch square of metallic silver paper
- [ ] 4-inch square of blue paper
- [ ] glue stick
- [ ] pin
- [ ] 6 metallic blue brads
- [ ] sewing needle
- [ ] golden embroidery floss
- [ ] scissors

1 Photocopy the star pattern on *page 155*, enlarging at 125 percent of the original size. Set the pattern aside.

2 Fold the white cardstock in half with short ends together. Glue the paper squares on top of one another as shown in photo. Do not glue to the card front yet.

3 Center the pattern on the blue paper square. Use pin to mark a hole at each outer point only. Use the holes as guides for placing the brads. Poke one brad through each hole and spread apart the prongs on the back side.

4 Thread the needle with embroidery floss and knot one end. Push the needle up from the back of the card squares, next to a brad. Wrap the floss around three of the brads to form a triangle. Wrap the brads a total of three times. Push the needle back through the starter hole and secure with a knot. Clip the floss end. Repeat for the other three brads. Glue the card squares to the front of the white card.

stamped with

The post office issues new stamps every year in celebration of Kwanzaa. Use these miniature masterpieces to get your happy gatherings under way.

table treats

❧ Beribboned treat cups and felt place mats set the table with style. Colorful stripes (inspired by last year's leftover postage stamps) unify the look.

What You'll Need...

- 2-inch flat round wooden disk
- black paint
- paintbrush
- self-adhesive ribbons in black and colors to coordinate with postage stamp
- scissors
- round container
- large colored wooden bead (available with children's toys)
- hot-glue gun and glue sticks

To make the treat cup

1 Paint the round wood disk black. Let the paint dry.

2 Cut short ribbon strips and press onto round container until surface is covered. Adhere a length of black ribbon around the rim.

3 Hot-glue the bead in the center of the black disk. Hot-glue the round container on top of the bead.

What You'll Need...

- felt sheets in colors to coordinate with postage stamp
- scissors
- straight pins
- 12×18-inch piece of black felt
- sewing machine
- black thread

To make the place mat

1 Cut a ½×12-inch strip from each sheet of colored felt.

2 Pin the felt strips side by side on one end of the black felt rectangle.

3 Machine-stitch the felt pieces to the background in a big zigzag fashion.

4 Cut the felt strips at different angles between the stitching to create texture.

assigned seating

❧ It's fun to look around a table and find the place that was reserved just for you. These vivid place cards tout guests' names with easy-to-read adhesive letters. Use a postage stamp on each one and a snippet of self-adhesive ribbon as graphic accents.

inspiration

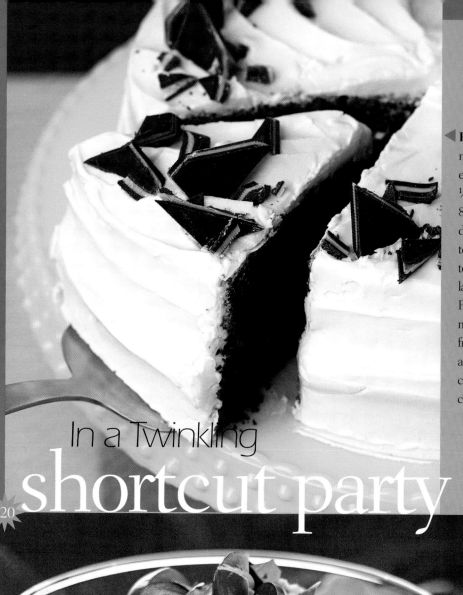

Crème de Menthe Showpiece

Prepare a two-layer chocolate cake mix according to package directions, except replace ¼ cup of the water with ¼ cup crème de menthe. Bake in two 8- or 9-inch round cake pans and cool as directed. Warm ½ cup fudge ice cream topping just until spreadable. Spread topping on the bottom side of one cake layer. Top with the second cake layer. For frosting, stir 1 tablespoon crème de menthe into a 16-ounce can of vanilla frosting. If desired, tint the frosting with a few drops of green food coloring. Frost cake. Garnish with coarsely chopped chocolate-mint candies.

In a Twinkling
shortcut party foods

Cheater's Guacamole

In a bowl combine ½ of a 16-ounce package (1 pouch) refrigerated guacamole (about 1 cup); 1 ripe avocado, halved, seeded, peeled, and coarsely chopped; 1½ teaspoons chopped chipotle pepper in adobo sauce; and ¼ teaspoon ground cumin. Top with quartered grape tomatoes, sliced ripe olives, and snipped fresh cilantro. Serve immediately with tortilla chips or vegetable dippers.

Appetizer Sampler with Lime-Chive Dip

◀ **For dip,** combine two 8-ounce containers dairy sour cream chive-flavor dip, ½ teaspoon finely shredded lime peel, and 1 tablespoon lime juice. Cover; chill for up to 24 hours. Serve with assorted dippers, such as whole wheat pita bread wedges; cherry tomatoes; baby carrots; broccoli florets; assorted crackers; sesame breadsticks; cooked small shrimp; thick-sliced salami, pepperoni, or summer sausage; and/or thick-sliced cheddar or provolone cheese cut into star shapes.

Mexican Shrimp Cocktail

▶ **In a bowl** toss together 1 pound cooked peeled and deveined large shrimp (leave tails on shrimp, if desired), 1 cup chunky salsa, 1 tablespoon lime juice, and 1 tablespoon snipped fresh cilantro. Cover; refrigerate for 2 to 4 hours. Transfer shrimp to a serving bowl. Sprinkle top with chopped avocado and garnish with lime wedges and cilantro sprigs.

121

Nut, Fruit, and Stilton Pita Pizzas

◀ **Split four pita bread rounds** in half horizontally. Toast, cut sides up, on baking sheets in a 350°F oven for 3 to 4 minutes. Cool slightly. Brush with olive oil (about 3 tablespoons total). Sprinkle each with ¼ cup purchased dried fruit and nut snack mix (such as a mixture of dried fruits, cashew pieces, dry-roasted peanuts, pumpkin seeds, sunflower seeds, and/or almonds). Top each with 3 tablespoons crumbled Stilton or other blue cheese. Bake at 350°F for 4 to 5 minutes or until cheese softens. Sprinkle each with ¼ teaspoon finely shredded lemon peel and 1 tablespoon finely shredded Parmesan or Romano cheese. Cut each into six wedges. Serve warm or at room temperature.

new year's fun

Ring in the New Year with friends and family by enjoying a night of board games. Set up a variety of stations throughout the house so guests can choose their favorite competition. Look to the game pieces for inspiration on how to decorate each table.

come out and play

❧ Turn to scrapbooking supplies to craft winning invitations. Stickers with a game theme make it easy. Decide whether you want them all the same or individualized to the players' favorite games.

playful greetings

❧ Guests will know they're in for a night of fun when greeted by this sparkling wreath. Start with an iced-twig wreath, adding ornaments and bows in red, silver, black, and white. Cut a piece of cardstock slightly larger than the wreath's center and use adhesive letters to add New Year's sentiments.

all decked out

❧ Go graphic with playing cards as your table decor. Glue the cards, faces out, on red painted boxes to hold snacks. To make playing card coasters, overlap two cards (2s and 8s) to make a square, adding adhesive 0s between the 2 and 8 to record the new year. Take the playing card squares to your local photocopy center for lamination. Use coordinating eyelets in the corners to adhere them to a cardstock backing.

& games

seeing spots

Play fair and you'll get to bring home this New Year's prize. A round 1-inch punch helps you make dots by the dozens. Place them domino-style on rectangular gift bags divided by a marking pen line. Fill the bags with salty or sweet treats.

check it out

Library card sleeves are the key to these party handouts. Available in school and teacher supply stores, the sleeves are just the right size to hold a deck of cards or large candy bar. Tie on a candy cane with ribbon and add some fresh holly for a clever presentation.

let the good times roll

The dice game table will draw young and old alike with lollipops calling their names. Painted wooden blocks have a hole drilled in the centers so the suckers stand on their own. Not only do the treat stands look cute, but they also hold the candy when it's your turn to roll.

125

GIVING *from the* HEART

Get ready to spread loads of holiday cheer! You'll feel like Santa himself delivering thoughtful surprises specially tailored for everyone on your gift list.

Cheese Straws

128

good things— in all kinds

Cheese Straws

Arrive with an armful of goodies at your next holiday party. Offer these luscious breadsticks to share once there and tell the hostess she can keep the container as a gift. Note that these should be enjoyed the same day they're baked.

- 1 17¼-ounce package frozen puff pastry, thawed (2 sheets)
- 1 egg white, lightly beaten
- 1 teaspoon cracked black pepper
- 1½ cups shredded dill Havarti cheese or Monterey Jack cheese with jalapeño peppers

Line two baking sheets with parchment paper; set aside.

Preheat oven to 375°F. Unfold pastry onto a lightly floured surface; brush lightly with some of the egg white. Sprinkle lightly with half of the pepper. Sprinkle with half of the cheese. Top with the second sheet of puff pastry. Brush with egg white and sprinkle with remaining pepper and cheese.

With a rolling pin, roll puff pastry to seal the sheets together and press cheese into the pastry.

Cut the pastry into long, ½-inch-wide strips. Gently twist each strip several times. (If desired, cut strips in half.) Transfer to prepared baking sheets, pressing down ends. Bake one sheet of cheese straws at a time for 18 to 20 minutes or until golden brown. Transfer to a wire rack and let cool. Makes about 20 breadsticks.

TO PRESENT AS SHOWN: Display breadsticks in a tall hurricane glass.

Asian Pineapple Cream Cheese Spread

Cilantro, chili-garlic sauce, and lime juice make this cheese spread irresistible!

- 3 8-ounce packages cream cheese, softened
- 2 tablespoons packed brown sugar
- 2 tablespoons lime juice
- 2 tablespoons Asian chili sauce
- 1 20-ounce can crushed pineapple, drained
- ¼ cup sliced green onion
- ¼ cup snipped fresh cilantro
- 1 teaspoon grated fresh ginger
  Assorted crackers

In a large mixing bowl beat cream cheese with an electric mixer on medium speed until smooth. Beat in brown sugar, lime juice, and chili sauce until combined. Stir in pineapple, onion, cilantro, and ginger. For gift giving, divide the spread evenly among six 10-ounce containers. Cover and chill for 2 hours or up to 3 days.

Wrap containers, tie with ribbon, and give with crackers as gifts. Makes 6 containers of spread.

TO PRESENT AS SHOWN: Use a silver chenille stem to attach a ribbon bow and small jingle bells to the lid of a glass sugar bowl. Present the container of spread with a box of crackers in a gift bag.

129

What do you give those friends who have everything?
Beautifully packaged homemade foods to make the season merry.

of packages

Cocoa Spiced Pecans

Cocoa Spiced Pecans

✳

Thanks to a combination of chocolate and just a little heat, nut lovers will go nuts for these treats.

1 egg white
1 teaspoon water
5 cups pecan halves
1 cup sugar
1 tablespoon unsweetened cocoa powder
1 teaspoon salt
½ teaspoon cayenne pepper

Preheat oven to 325°F. Grease two 15×10×1-inch baking pans; set aside.
In a large bowl beat egg white and water together until combined. Add pecans and toss to coat.
In a small bowl combine sugar, cocoa powder, salt, and cayenne pepper. Sprinkle the sugar mixture over pecans and toss to coat.
Spread half of the pecans in each prepared baking pan. Bake one pan for 20 minutes. Spread nuts on waxed paper; cool. If necessary, break into individual nut halves. Repeat with remaining nuts.

Divide coated nuts among six small airtight bags or containers. Store the pecans for up to 2 weeks at room temperature or freeze for longer storage. Makes 6 (1-cup) gifts.
TO PRESENT AS SHOWN: Glue holiday fabric to a cardboard cone and embellish the lip with feathery trim. Use an ice pick to make a hole in each side of the cone; thread with ribbon, knotting the ribbon on the inside. Fill icing bags with the nuts and tie bags closed with another ribbon. Nestle the bags inside the decorated cones.

Sublime Wine Crackers

Sublime Wine Crackers

- 1 cup all-purpose flour
- ¼ cup snipped fresh basil
- 2 tablespoons pine nuts, finely ground
- ½ teaspoon salt
- ⅛ to ¼ teaspoon ground black pepper
- 3 tablespoons Sauvignon Blanc
- 2 tablespoons olive oil
  Kosher salt

Preheat oven to 325°F. In a bowl combine flour, basil, pine nuts, salt, and pepper. In a small bowl combine wine and oil; gradually add to flour mixture, tossing with a fork until combined. Form dough into a ball. (Dough will appear dry but will come together when gently worked. Avoid adding more liquid; this can result in tough crackers.)

Transfer dough to a lightly floured surface. Roll into a 12×9-inch rectangle about ⅛ to 1⁄16 inch thick (trim uneven edges, if necessary). Prick dough all over with a fork. Using a pastry wheel, cut dough into 3×1½-inch rectangles. Gently transfer rectangles to an ungreased baking sheet and sprinkle with kosher salt.

Bake about 18 minutes or just until crackers start to brown and are firm to the touch. Transfer to wire racks; cool completely. Store in airtight container at room temperature up to 1 week or freeze up to 3 months. Makes 24 crackers.

TO PRESENT AS SHOWN: Place the crackers in a cellophane-lined take-out container. Wrap the handle with a red metallic chenille stem and finish with a coordinating purchased trim.

Gracious Gift Giving

Keep these tips in mind when giving food gifts:

- **Choose the proper container and materials:** Make sure any container you use to store, package, or present food is nontoxic and food-safe.
- **Offer serving suggestions:** It might help to print a little gift tag that explains what the gift is and how to best enjoy it.
- **Be sure to pass along storage instructions** to the recipients to allow them to safely store the food if they do not eat it right away.

Orange and Chocolate Chip Shortbread

TO PRESENT AS SHOWN: Glue miniature house ornaments to white box lids. Line the boxes with tissue to cushion the shortbread.

132

Orange and Chocolate Chip Shortbread

Chocolate chips enhance the delicate citrus flavor of these cookies. Dark chocolate chips would be an equally good substitute.

  1 cup butter, softened
  ½ cup granulated sugar
  2 teaspoons finely shredded
      orange peel
2¼ cups all-purpose flour
  ¾ cup miniature semisweet
      chocolate pieces
  1 recipe Orange Glaze

Preheat oven to 325°F. In a medium mixing bowl beat butter with an electric mixer on medium to high speed for 30 seconds. Add sugar and orange peel. Beat until combined, scraping sides of bowl occasionally. Add flour and beat until crumbly. Stir in the chocolate pieces with a wooden spoon, pressing dough together until smooth.

On an ungreased cookie sheet, press dough into a 12×8-inch rectangle (about ¼ inch thick). Bake for 25 to 30 minutes or until bottom just begins to brown and center is set. Cool on cookie sheet on a wire rack. Spread Orange Glaze over shortbread. Let stand at least 30 minutes until glaze is set. Cut lengthwise into three strips. Cut each strip crosswise into eight pieces, making 24 rectangles. Cut each rectangle lengthwise into two pieces. Makes 48 cookies.

ORANGE GLAZE: In a small bowl whisk together ½ cup powdered sugar, 1 tablespoon softened butter, and 1 tablespoon orange juice. If necessary, whisk in additional orange juice, 1 teaspoon at a time, until glaze reaches desired consistency.

TO STORE: Place cookies in layers separated by waxed paper in an airtight container; cover and store at room temperature for up to 3 days. Or freeze uncut shortbread for up to 3 months; thaw, glaze, and cut shortbread.

Chocolate-Cashew Bread

Chocolate-Cashew Bread

You also can present this luscious bread with a pound of gourmet coffee!

  2 cups all-purpose flour
  ½ cup sugar
  1 tablespoon baking powder
  ½ teaspoon salt
  1 egg
  ¾ cup milk
  ½ cup cooking oil
1⅓ cups semisweet chocolate pieces
  1 cup chopped cashews or
      hazelnuts (filberts)
  ½ teaspoon shortening
      Coarsely chopped or whole
      cashews or hazelnuts (filberts)
      (optional)

Preheat oven to 350°F. Grease bottom and ½ inch up the sides of six 4½×2½×1½-inch loaf pans;* set aside. In a large bowl stir together flour, sugar, baking powder, and salt. Make a well in center of flour mixture; set aside.

In a medium bowl beat egg with a fork; stir in milk and oil. Add egg mixture all at once to flour mixture. Stir just until moistened (batter should be lumpy). Fold in 1 cup of the chocolate pieces and 1 cup cashews.

Divide batter among prepared pans; spread evenly. Bake for 35 to 40 minutes or until a wooden toothpick inserted near the center comes out clean. Cool in pans on wire rack for 10 minutes. Remove from pans. Cool completely on wire rack. Wrap and store overnight.

Before serving, in a heavy small saucepan combine remaining ⅓ cup chocolate pieces and shortening. Heat and stir over low heat until melted and smooth. Drizzle chocolate mixture over loaves. If desired, sprinkle additional nuts on top. Let stand until chocolate is set. Makes 6 mini loaves.

*NOTE: Instead of the six small loaf pans, you can make one large or three medium-size loaves. Spoon batter into one 8×4×2-inch loaf pan or divide batter among three 7½×3½×2-inch loaf pans. Bake in a 350°F oven for 50 to 55 minutes for one large loaf or 35 to 40 minutes for three medium loaves. Cool, store, and garnish as above.

TO PRESENT AS SHOWN: Place the bread on a holiday plate, wrap, and tie with pretty ribbon and a holiday pick.

133

decked-out desk

Map paper in rich jewel tones gives these accessories a masculine look. All it takes is a change of scrapbook paper and these useful containers could be for anyone, any age.

What You'll Need...

- cork memo board
- 2 octagonal papier-mâché boxes
- pencil holder
- small letter holder
- scissors
- brown suede scrapbook paper
- map scrapbook paper
- wallpaper or scrapbook paper in tan and burgundy
- spray glue
- tan grosgrain ribbon
- fabric tack glue
- 16 wooden ball feet
- copper paint
- paintbrush
- crafts glue
- drill
- 4 antiqued brass knobs
- 1 washer to fit brass knob
- 2 copper insertible name plate brackets
- alphabet stickers in black or brown

office essentials

The men in your life will thank you again and again for these handsome office organizers.

1 Using the photograph and your office items as guides, cut wallpaper and/or scrapbook papers to fit. Use spray glue to affix papers to each desk set item.

2 Embellish the desk accessories by gluing grosgrain ribbon onto each item with fabric glue.

3 Paint the wooden ball feet with copper. Let dry. Use crafts glue to adhere four painted wooden ball feet to the bottom of each papier-mâché box, the letter holder, and the pencil holder. Space the balls evenly so each box sits flat.

4 Drill a hole in the center of the smaller of the papier-mâché box lids for the brass knob. Screw the antiqued brass knob to the small box lid for a decorative handle, using a washer on the inside of the lid so the knob doesn't pull through.

5 Drill three evenly spaced holes along the wooden frame at the bottom edge of the memo board. Screw knobs into the holes.

6 Use crafts glue to attach copper brackets to the memo board and letter holder. Cut a paper scrap to fit into each bracket. Before inserting, label each one using alphabet stickers. Insert the papers into the brackets.

fun for the cook

136

The butcher, the baker, the cookie maker —
everyone seems to spend his or her share of time in the hub of the
house. These gifts will make it a pleasure to be there.

blooming beauty

～ Dimensional button flowers and beaded polka dots coat a plain white recipe box with cheerful bursts of color. Start your cook off right by including a few recipe cards that have been decorated with easy-to-find scrapbooking materials.

What You'll Need...

- ☐ black enamel acrylic paint
- ☐ disposable plate
- ☐ small flat paintbrush
- ☐ white recipe box
- ☐ buttons in green and assorted colors, shapes, and sizes, including hearts and circles
- ☐ toothpick
- ☐ strong adhesive, such as E6000
- ☐ small tube beads and seed beads

1 Place a small amount of black paint onto a disposable plate. Paint a frame around the front of the recipe box. Let the paint dry.

2 On a flat surface arrange buttons to create three flowers for the front of the box and one each for the sides and top of the box. Place the green buttons by the flowers to appear as leaves.

3 Use a toothpick and adhesive to adhere the buttons to the box. Let dry.

4 Add dimension with more layers of buttons and beads, working from largest to smallest. Adhere bead polka dots to the painted frame area. Let dry.

the finish line

～ A variety of coordinating ribbons and fabric ruffles dress up tea towels in a jiffy. Simply cut the trims slightly longer than the width of the towel end, then topstitch the strips in place.

sweet sensation

❧ Treat your baking buddies to hot pads that are as sweet as they are. Even if you're new to patchwork, you can whip up this easy checkerboard design. Choose a striped fabric for the center to ease handstitching.
NOTE: Measurements include ¼-inch seam allowance. Stitch with right sides facing.

What You'll Need...

- fabric scissors
- tape measure
- 2×20-inch piece of red dot fabric
- 2×20-inch piece of yellow dot fabric
- 5×8-inch piece of striped fabric
- 8×10-inch piece of backing fabric
- embroidery floss in contrasting color
- embroidery needle
- 8×10-inch piece of batting
- assorted beads
- thread

1 Cut the following:
Ten 1¾-inch squares of red dot fabric
Ten 1¾-inch squares of yellow dot fabric
3x6¾-inch piece of striped fabric

2 Cut a fabric loop from backing fabric. Piece squares around center striped fabric according to diiagram on *page 154*.

3 Using embroidery floss, embroider "Sweet Treats" as desired. Stitch and baste fabric loop to top left corner of patchwork.

4 Line patchwork with batting. Stitch front to backing, right sides facing. Stitch around outside edge leaving an opening for turning. Trim batting and backing to ¼-inch seam allowance. Trim corners; turn to right side and press. Sew on beads.

sprinkled with love

❧ An oversize cupcake shape is the perfect ingredient for this hot pad. Top it with glass bead sprinkles and a fabric cherry to complete the look.

What You'll Need...

- 8×10-inch piece of fusible webbing; iron
- pencil
- fabric scissors
- 10-inch square of background fabric
- 5×8-inch piece of turquoise fabric
- 5×9-inch piece of yellow dot fabric
- 6×8-inch piece of orange and yellow striped fabric
- 3×4-inch piece of red fabric
- matching threads
- 10-inch square of backing fabric
- 10-inch square of batting
- tape measure
- sewing needle
- assorted glass beads

1 Enlarge and trace pattern pieces from *page 154* onto fusible webbing according to manufacturer's instructions. Cut out and fuse, centering the design onto the background fabric.

2 Machine-appliqué around the pieces using a close zigzag stitch and matching threads. Cut and stitch a fabric loop from backing fabric. Baste loop to top of cherry.

3 Line the appliqué design with batting. With right sides facing, stitch front to backing fabric ⅛ inch past the design, leaving an opening for turning. Cut out design, leaving a ¼-inch seam allowance. Clip into seam allowance for easy turning. Turn to right side. Press and stitch opening closed. Sew on beads.

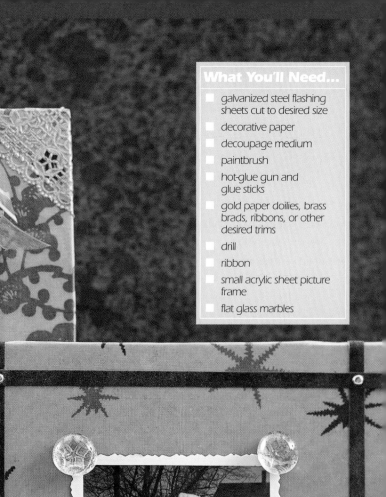

What You'll Need...

- galvanized steel flashing sheets cut to desired size
- decorative paper
- decoupage medium
- paintbrush
- hot-glue gun and glue sticks
- gold paper doilies, brass brads, ribbons, or other desired trims
- drill
- ribbon
- small acrylic sheet picture frame
- flat glass marbles

140

Family and friends will love showing off their favorite photos in frames and books that are as beautiful as the memories they hold.

giving memories

stick to it

〰 With a steel backing and decorative magnets, it's easy to swap out photos in these pretty tabletop frames. NOTE: You can use precut galvanized steel sheets that come in 5×7-inch rectangles or you can cut your own to the desired size. Precut rectangles overlapped several times created the sizes shown. The frames featured are 7-inch square and 7×9-inch rectangle.

1 Cover the steel frames with decorative paper using several coats of decoupage medium following the manufacturer's instructions.

2 Embellish the frames by gluing on coordinating scrapbook papers, gold paper doilies, ribbons, or brass brads to create a border.

3 For a hanging frame drill two holes in the center of the top of the frame and tie sheer ribbons in a bow. For a frame that is placed on a table, glue a small acrylic sheet frame to the bottom edge of the back of the steel frame. The acrylic sheet frame will act as a base for the magnetic frame.

4 Using decoupage medium, glue circles of coordinating paper onto the back of flat decorative clear marbles, creating four for each frame.

5 Once the decoupage medium is dry, glue a craft magnet onto the back of each of the embellished marbles. The decorative magnetic marbles will hold your pictures in place on the steel frames.

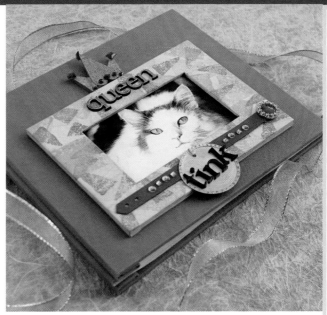

clever cover

〰 Here's a photo album cover that's purr-fect for the kitty (or doggy!) lovers on your holiday list. Scrapbooking supplies personalize the cover.

1 If you purchased a paintable flat frame, paint it soft lime green first. Leave the sample paper inside the frame while you paint it, then throw away when paint is dry.

2 Put small dabs of turquoise, baby blue, and lavender paint onto a disposable plate. Cut a sponge into small squares and triangles, soak sponge pieces in water, and squeeze out excess. Press sponge into paint and press random patterns onto the painted frame. Repeat with all colors until the frame is painted as desired. Let dry.

3 Trim braid or ribbon to fit the frame. Trim one end with a point. Trim the other end an extra ½ inch to allow for the buckle. Insert one end of braid or ribbon into the buckle, fold over ½ inch, and glue in place with adhesive. Let dry.

4 On a piece of newspaper, lay down the smaller hearts first (upside down) and place the larger heart upside down on top of the smaller pair. Glue the three together with adhesive. Let dry.

5 Paint the heart crown with a gold paint pen. Paint the tag with a gold paint pen. Let dry.

6 Tie a gold cord into the hole on the tag. Use a toothpick to glue dimensional letters onto the tag. Glue letters onto the top portion of the frame, if you wish. Let dry. Add little dots of gold glitter paint around the edge of tag. Let dry.

7 Use adhesive-backed gems to decorate the collar and crown. If desired, enhance the lettering with gold paint pen, just painting the top surface.

8 Use adhesive to apply the collar and tag to the bottom portion of the frame. Let dry.

9 Insert a photo into the frame. Use a generous amount of adhesive to apply the frame to the album cover. Glue crown at top center of frame. Let dry.

What You'll Need...

- ☐ newspaper
- ☐ paintable flat frame (available in scrapbook or craft section of crafts store)
- ☐ acrylic paints in lime green, turquoise, baby blue, and lavender
- ☐ paintbrush
- ☐ disposable plate
- ☐ flat painting sponge
- ☐ water
- ☐ braid or ribbon for collar
- ☐ scissors
- ☐ tiny buckle (available in scrapbook, sewing notions, or button section of store)
- ☐ strong adhesive, such as E6000
- ☐ 3 wooden hearts to make crown
- ☐ gold paint pen
- ☐ paper tag with hole
- ☐ gold cord
- ☐ dimensional letters
- ☐ toothpick
- ☐ glitter gold paint
- ☐ adhesive-backed gems
- ☐ small photo album

miniskirt purse

Think twice before you toss out an outgrown denim skirt or head to the nearest garage sale or thrift shop to find one. Stitch the bottom of skirt front and back together with beaded trim sandwiched between. Attach purchased handles to belt loops and tack butterfly trim to the pocket for a purse that any girl will love flinging over her shoulder.

142

bag a great gift

Kids score big time when they unwrap a one-of-a-kind denim purse or duffel bag. Hide little gifts in the pockets for extra smiles.

cool denim duffel

Whether off to a sleepover or to softball practice, kids find this duffel a necessity. Sewn from last year's denim, the slightly ragged look is right in style.

What You'll Need...

- jeans
- tape measure
- fabric scissors
- 16-inch heavy-duty zipper
- 2 bungee cords with plastic hooks for handles
- assorted purchased items to hang from handle, such as key holders, padlock, mini flashlight, etc.
- sewing maching; thread

1 Square up jeans front and back to a width approximately 16 inches across. Cut and piece together as necessary the jeans fabric to form a rectangle approximately 16×36 inches. The waistband plus pockets of the jeans must be at each end of rectangle. Cut two 12-inch circles from leg of jeans for the ends of the duffel bag.

2 Attach top zipper onto each end of fabric rectangle; stitch in place. Stitch a circle of fabric onto each end of duffel bag using ¼-inch seams and right sides facing.

3 Attach bungee cords with hook ends into belt loops for handles. Hang accessories from the loops.

143

Go with the Green ▶
Expect big hugs from college kids when they receive desk items filled with always needed money. Wrap bills around pencils or pens for a two-in-one gift. This creative presentation is so much more fun than tucking cash in an envelope and leaves room for coins as well as holiday candies.

In a Twinkling

gifts to give

◀ **Popcorn and a Movie** Choose a DVD and use it as a theme to create a gift "basket" for an entire family. Bowls, drinks, popcorn, decorative salt and pepper shakers, and candy will provide an extra special evening of family entertainment.

Baby, It's Cold Outside Warm up your little sweetheart with a jar of hot chocolate mix topped with a pretty holiday bow. Purchase coordinating mittens and a furry friend so your youngster can play, drink, and be merry!

145

Sweet Indulgence Ice cream fanatics will love new bowls with their favorite toppings nestled inside. Choose plastic bowls that are tall enough to hold a topping jar when placed one on top of the other. As a bonus include a gift certificate to the recipient's favorite creamery.

What a Trip Know someone who's planning a special vacation? Use the destination as a theme and gather small items, such as a photo album, scrapbooking embellishments, and a disposable camera, to fill a mini suitcase gift box.

JUST *for* KIDS

Let kids in on the fun of crafting projects they'll be proud to make and share with the people they love. You'll feed their artistic nature while reinforcing that it is better to give.

silly stuff

Glued, tied, and twisted, these projects keep little ones busy for hours. With inexpensive supplies they can make enough for everyone!

write on

These fancy pencil toppers stand on their own as stocking stuffers, or tuck them between the ribbons on holiday packages.

What You'll Need...
- feathers
- colored pencils
- floral tape
- crafts glue
- ½-inch grosgrain ribbon in a variety of colors
- ⅛-inch ribbon in a variety of colors cut into 12-inch strips

1 Attach desired feathers to the top of each pencil by wrapping with floral tape.

2 Once the feathers are attached as desired, use crafts glue to cover the floral tape with coordinating grosgrain ribbon.

3 For additional decoration tie a ribbon bow around the grosgrain ribbon.

potato-print snowmen

Turn kids' imaginations loose with bright pipe cleaners, pom-poms, and feathers to build all kinds of fancily clad snow characters.

What You'll Need...

- newspaper
- knife
- potato
- cutting board
- cardstock
- scissors
- paper trimmer
- decorative-edge scissors
- small suckers
- clear tape
- white acrylic paint
- disposable plate
- pencil with eraser end
- cardboard
- grommet punch
- small hammer
- adhesive glue dots
- pipe cleaners
- plastic eyes
- tiny and medium-size pom-poms
- crafts glue
- cabochons
- feathers
- glue stick

1 Cover the work surface with newspaper. Ask an adult to use a cutting board and cut a potato in half with a smooth, straight cut.

2 For each snowman, using a paper trimmer, scissors, or decorative-edge scissors, trim a piece of cardstock 2 inches longer and 3 inches wider than the sucker. If the sucker has printing on one side, place the clear side of the wrapper faceup on the card. Tape the extra plastic wrapper around the edges to the back for a smooth edge.

3 Place some white acrylic paint on a disposable plate. Press the potato into the paint and move it around a little. Practice printing circles onto the newspaper. When happy with the results, stamp the trimmed cardstock with a circle of paint centered and approximately 1 inch from the bottom of the paper as shown in Photo A, *right*. Let dry.

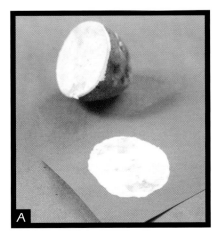

A

4 Position the sucker on the printed paper. With a pencil mark a dot on each side of the stick for the pipe cleaner scarf as shown in Photo B.

5 Place the paper on the cardboard with the cutting board underneath. Ask an adult to place the grommet punch onto each mark and pound with a small hammer until two holes are punched as shown in Photo C.

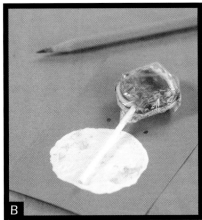

B

6 Use a glue dot on the back of the sucker to attach it to the card for a snowman head. Pull one or two pipe cleaners through the holes and twist as desired for a scarf as shown in Photo D. Use glue dots to add plastic eyes and a pom-pom nose.

7 Put a dab of crafts glue on the plate. Dip tiny pom-poms or cabochons in the glue and add to the stick for buttons. Dip the larger pom-poms in glue and add for hat. Do the same with a feather.

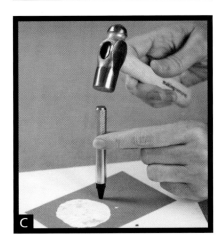

C

8 Trim a second piece of cardstock as a backing or folded card. Make it slightly larger than the first card. Use a glue stick to glue the snowman card onto the bigger piece of cardstock.

9 Add snowflakes to the card by dipping the eraser end of a pencil in white paint and dotting it onto the paper.

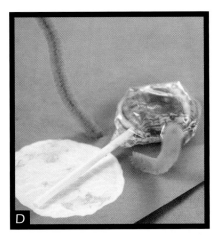

D

tiny town
of treats

A quick trip to the candy shop is all it takes
to gather supplies for this fun-to-make village. Kids will have a blast
creating a snowy scene that glistens on a sugared mirror.

What You'll Need...

- waxed paper
- disposable plates
- graham crackers
- frostings in chocolate, vanilla, and green in tube
- knife
- corn syrup
- pastry brush
- sugars in red and green
- chocolate and colored sprinkles
- chocolate-covered wafer bars
- sugar wafer cookies
- sugar cones
- toothpick
- frosting in cans with decorative tips (optional)
- edible trims, such as decorative cake sprinkles, chocolate and fruit-flavored candies, chocolate bars, gummy ribbon candy, tiny cookies, oblong sandwich cookies, birthday candleholders, birthday candles, and marshmallows

santa land

Your little ones can create a centerpiece everyone will enjoy. This sugary village looks just as snowy as the North Pole.

1 Cover the work surface with waxed paper. Have several disposable plates ready to use.

2 Use graham crackers whole or break them into squares or rectangles as needed. Stack and use frosting as the glue. Stack the pieces first without frosting so you know what shapes you will need.

3 To make a solid base for a building, stack enough graham crackers to make a cube. Spread a little frosting between each, just in the center to make them stick together as shown in Photo A, *right*. The base has to be at least half as high as the walls will be.

4 For the red barn pour a small amount of corn syrup onto a plate and use a pastry brush to spread a very thin coat over the crackers you want to be red. Sprinkle with red sugar. Set aside.

5 For the roofs spread cracker tops with a thin layer of chocolate frosting, covering the edges. Shake chocolate sprinkles or colored sprinkles onto the wet frosting. Set aside.

6 Assemble the walls and roofs using frosting between pieces. To make the peaked walls, turn a square graham cracker at an angle and stick it to the end as shown in Photo B.

7 For the church make a rectangular base from 12 chocolate-covered wafer bars. Spread frosting on the top bars and cover with graham crackers for a flat roof.

8 To make the steeple, stick two sugar wafer cookies together with frosting. Add frosting to both ends. Stick one end into a sugar cone, the other end on the rooftop. Frost the edges of the crackers to make a roof and add it to the top.

9 For trees paint cones with a coat of corn syrup; sprinkle with green sugar.

10 To trim trees and buildings, use tube frosting and apply decorations with a knife or toothpick. You can also use frosting that comes in a can with different tips.

11 For doors and windows use flat small cookies or crackers and use chocolate bars for steps. Attach with contrasting frosting so it oozes out around the edges.

12 To make stained-glass windows, spread frosting onto tiny cookie treats and dip in sprinkles. Then add to the building.

13 Trim the trees and buildings as desired. Let set before moving.

151

A

B

too, too cute

Kids will grin ear to ear making these jolly cups and ornaments. In fact they're so cool, they'll be a hit at the next neighborhood craft boutique.

152

What You'll Need...

- ceramic mug
- disposable plate
- glass paints, such as Liquitex Glossies, in red, white, green, and yellow
- pencil with new eraser
- toothpick

christmas cups

A coffee cup for a teacher? A hot chocolate mug for a friend? No matter! Kids crave making these quick gifts using a painting technique that doesn't even require a brush.

1 Wash the mug and let it dry. Avoid touching the areas to be painted.

2 Put a small amount of each desired paint color on a disposable plate. To make the large dots, dip the pencil eraser in paint and dot on the mug using the photograph, *opposite*, as a guide. To make small dots, dip the pencil point or a toothpick in paint and dot onto the mug. Let the paint dry. If recommended by the paint manufacturer, bake the mug in the oven according to the directions.

What You'll Need...

- waxed paper
- rolling pin
- oven-bake clay, such as Sculpey, in red, green, and white
- millefiori beads in holiday themes
- scissors and decorative-edge scissors
- baking sheet
- strong glue, such as E6000
- crafts wire
- wire cutters
- round-nose pliers
- small seed beads in black and white
- large seed beads in black and white
- ceramic beads in colors to coordinate with millefiori beads

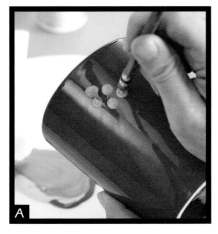

A

B

funky clay ornaments

Baking an ornament? Of course! You'll teach kids how to hone their cookie-making skills by making sweet little ornaments that require rolling, cutting out, and baking.

1 Place a piece of waxed paper on a flat work surface. Using one clay at a time, roll out a quarter of each color to sheets approximately ⅛ inch thick.

2 Press a millefiori bead lightly into the center of a clay sheet. Use scissors or decorative-edge scissors to trim around the bead, leaving a small border. Lay the clay shape on a contrasting color of clay and repeat the process.

3 Remove the beads and set them aside. Carefully separate the clay pieces and put them on a baking sheet. With an adult's help, bake the clay in the oven according to the manufacturer's instructions. Let cool.

4 Use adhesive to glue the clay pieces and millefiori bead together. Let the adhesive dry.

5 Cut a 12-inch piece of wire. Use round-nose pliers to make a small ring at the bottom of one end of the wire. Thread on approximately 30 small seed beads, alternating black and white. Thread on a large seed bead and a ceramic bead. Push the wire through the millefiori bead. Place another ceramic bead and three small seed beads onto the wire end.

6 Use round-nose pliers to curl and twist the wire as desired. Twist the end into a small loop so beads cannot fall off.

project details

SPRINKLED WITH LOVE
HOT PAD
enlarge 200%
pages 138–139

SOCK TALK STOCKINGS
full-size pattern
pages 56–57

SOCK TALK STOCKINGS
enlarge 200%
pages 56–57

Sweet Treats

SWEET SENSATION HOT PAD
full-size pattern
page 138–139

Sweet
Treats

SWEET SENSATION
HOT PAD
Assembly Diagram
pages 138–139

SOCK TALK STOCKINGS
enlarge 200%
pages 56–57

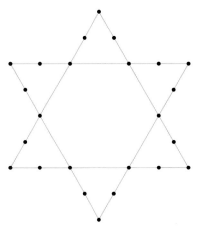

STUDDED STAR CANDLE
enlarge 200%
AND
WRAPPED IN GOLD CARD
enlarge 125%
pages 116–117

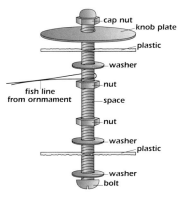

cap nut
knob plate
plastic
washer
fish line
from ornmament
nut
space
nut
washer
plastic
washer
bolt

FROSTY FRAME PICTURE
Knob/Screw Assembly
page 42

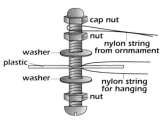

cap nut
nut
nylon string
from ornmament
washer
plastic
washer
nylon string
for hanging
nut

FROSTY FRAME PICTURE
Hanger Screw Assembly
page 42

155

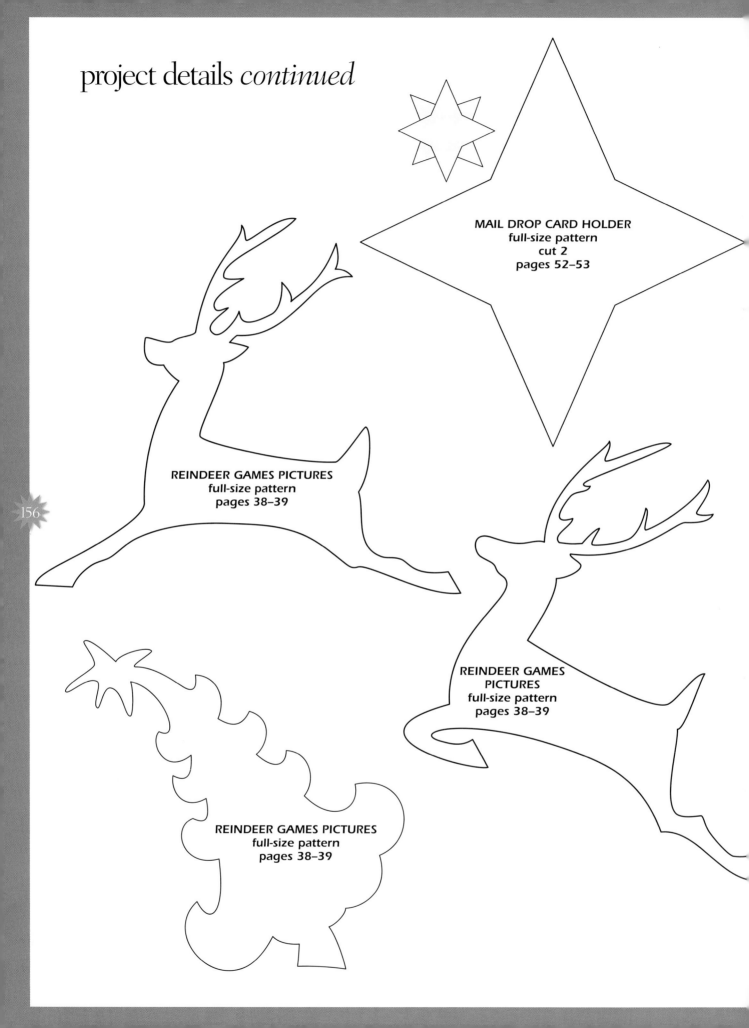

project details *continued*

MAIL DROP CARD HOLDER
full-size pattern
cut 2
pages 52–53

REINDEER GAMES PICTURES
full-size pattern
pages 38–39

REINDEER GAMES
PICTURES
full-size pattern
pages 38–39

REINDEER GAMES PICTURES
full-size pattern
pages 38–39

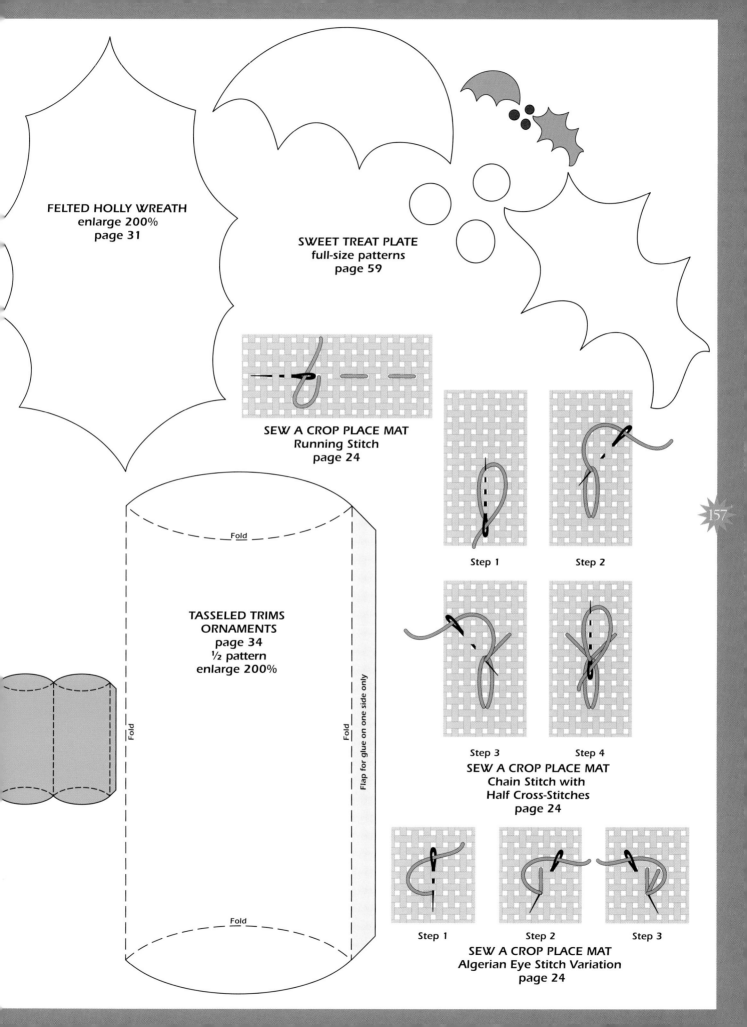

FELTED HOLLY WREATH
enlarge 200%
page 31

SWEET TREAT PLATE
full-size patterns
page 59

SEW A CROP PLACE MAT
Running Stitch
page 24

Fold

TASSELED TRIMS
ORNAMENTS
page 34
½ pattern
enlarge 200%

Fold

Fold

Flap for glue on one side only

Fold

Step 1

Step 2

Step 3

Step 4

SEW A CROP PLACE MAT
Chain Stitch with
Half Cross-Stitches
page 24

Step 1

Step 2

Step 3

SEW A CROP PLACE MAT
Algerian Eye Stitch Variation
page 24

project details *continued*

WARM AND WOOLLY THROW
page 80

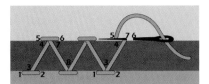

WARM AND WOOLLY THROW
Chevron Stitch
page 80

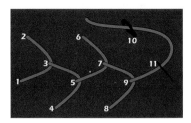

WARM AND WOOLLY THROW
Feather Stitch
page 80

WARM AND WOOLLY THROW
Blanket Stitch
page 80

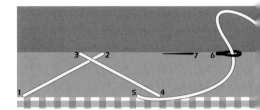

WARM AND WOOLLY THROW
Herringbone Stitch
page 80

WARM AND WOOLLY THROW
French Knot
page 80

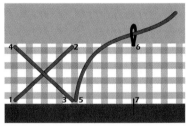

WARM AND WOOLLY THROW
Cross-Stitch
page 80

WINTER'S NAP PILLOWCASE
page 82

WINTER'S NAP PILLOWCASE
Chain Stitch
page 82

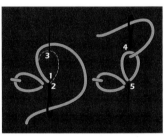

WINTER'S NAP PILLOWCASE
Lazy Daisy Stitch
page 82

WINTER'S NAP PILLOWCASE
Zigzag Stitch
page 82

WINTER'S NAP PILLOWCASE
Reverse Herringbone
page 82

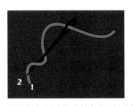

WINTER'S NAP PILLOWCASE
French Knot
page 82

index

index *continued*

RECIPES

A-D

E-L

M-P

R-Z

CREDITS & SOURCES

Unless otherwise stated,
photo styling by Catherine Brett
and Susan Banker. Food styling by
Janet Pittman.
Photographs by Jay Wilde.
cover: design, Sue Banker
page 4: design, Sue Banker
pages 8–9: design, Alice Wetzel
page 10: design, Rachel Sindelar; maple leaf
charms by Scrap Arts, scraparts.com or call
503/631-4893
pages 11–12: designs, Alice Wetzel
pages 14–17: Pomegranate Candlescape,
Beribboned Napkin Rings, and Let's Wheat
designs, Rachel Sindelar; Harvest Table Runner,
Margaret Sindelar
pages 18–19: design, Sue Banker
pages 20–23: designs, Alice Wetzel
pages 24–25: Sew a Crop and Raffia Wraps
designs, Rachel Sindelar; Mosaic Master and Go
with the Grain designs, Sue Banker; Pinecone
Tassel, Gayle Schadendorf
pages 26–29: designs, Alice Wetzel
pages 30–33: A Wreath with Presence design,
Carol Linnan; Felted Holly and Pinecone Star
designs, Rachel Sindelar; Drum Up Attention
and Merry Medallion designs, Sue Banker; Door
Decor design, Alice Wetzel
pages 34–37: Tasseled Trims and Tag, You're
It designs, Margaret Sindelar; Blooms and Bells
design, Rachel Sindelar; Festive Facets design,
Gayle Schadendorf; Blooms and Bells ribbon
by Midori, 708 6th Avenue North, Seattle, WA
98109, midoriribbon.com
pages 38–43: Reindeer Games and Frosty
Frame designs, Alice Wetzel; Merry and Bright,
Stretched to Fit, and Christmas Collage designs,
Sue Banker
pages 44–47: Photo styling, Kelsey Aikin
pages 48–49: Your Serve, String It On, and All
Aglow designs, Alice Wetzel; The Base of It All
and Lid It Up, Up, Up designs, Sue Banker
pages 50–53: Oh Night Divine, Worldly
Wishes, and Say It Like It Is designs, Sue Banker;
Mail Drop design, Alice Wetzel
pages 54–59: Stack 'Em, Sock Talk, and Baskets
of Fun designs, Margaret Sindelar; Good Sport
and Sweet Treat designs, Sue Banker; Stack 'Em
ribbon, The Beadery Craft Products, PO Box 178,
Hope Valley, RI 02832; Sock Talk wool by Weeks
Dye Works, 1510–103 Mechanical Boulevard,
Garner, NC 27529, weeksdyeworks.com
pages 60–61: Topiary Boulevard design, Rachel
Sindelar; Sparkling Mosaics and Starry, Starry
Night designs, Sue Banker
pages 62–63: Mini Masterpieces, Cookie Cutter,
and Impressive Wood Medallions designs, Sue
Banker; Sand Prints and No-Sew Special designs,
Gayle Schadendorf; Falling Snowflakes design,
Rachel Sindelar; Sand Prints sand by Activa
Products, Inc., activaproducts.com
pages 66–75: designs, Libby Becker and Breaca
Lozier of Special Arrangements; recipe developer:
Carrie E. Holcomb
pages 76–79: Photo styling, Kelsey Aikin
pages 80–83: Warm and Woolly, Winter's
Nap Pillowcase, and Jingle All the Way designs,
Margaret Sindelar; Life's Little Necessities design,
Sue Banker; Merry Mittens design, Rachel
Sindelar; Warm and Woolly throw trims, Wrights,
85 South Street, P.O. box 398, West Warren, MA
01092, wrights.com
pages 84–89: Recipe developer: Joyce Lock
pages 90–95: Feathers All Around and Leather
and Lace designs, Margaret Sindelar; Wild West
Trims, Ranch Wraps, Western Pine, and Holiday
Horseplay designs, Sue Banker
pages 96–109: Festive Fixture, Merry Manners,
Ring Around the Evergreen, and The Main
Man designs, Libby Becker and Breaca Lozier of
Special Arrangements; Take-Away Tree,
Sue Banker
pages 110–111: designs, Sue Banker
pages 116–119: designs, Sue Banker
pages 122–125: designs, Sue Banker
pages 128–133: designs, Sue Banker
pages 134–135: designs, Rachel Sindelar
pages 136–139: The Finish Line, Sweet
Sensation, and Sprinkled with Love designs,
Margaret Sindelar; Blooming Beauty design,
Alice Wetzel
pages 140–141: Stick to It design, Rachel
Sindelar; Clever Cover design, Alice Wetzel
pages 142–143: designs, Margaret Sindelar;
Miniskirt Purse handles, Bag Boutique, Prym-Dritz
Corporation, P.O. Box 5028, Spartanburg, SC
29304, dritz.com
pages 144–145: designs, Sue Banker
pages 148–149: Write On design, Rachel
Sindelar; Potato-Print Snowmen, Alice Wetzel
pages 150–151: designs, Alice Wetzel
pages 152–153: designs, Sue Banker